FROM TORONTO TO EMMAUS

FROM TORONTO TO EMMAUS

The Empty Tomb

And the Journey from Skepticism to Faith

James R. White

SOLID GROUND CHRISTIAN BOOKS
BIRMINGHAM, ALABAMA USA

Solid Ground Christian Books
715 Oak Grove Road
Homewood, AL 35209
205-443-0311
sgcb@charter.net
http://solid-ground-books.com

FROM TORONTO TO EMMAUS
The Empty Tomb and the Journey from Skepticism to Faith

James R. White

© Copyright James White 2007

Solid Ground Burning Issues Series

Cover design by Borgo Design
Contact them at borgogirl@bellsouth.net

ISBN 1-59925-112-4

Thanks and Dedication

Writing a book in sixteen days is a challenge. Writing one that delves into the wide variety of issues represented by the Talpiot tomb theory is even more so. A host of people have been vital to this lightning fast project. First, Rich Pierce and Marie Peterson were on board from the start. As soon as I decided to write this book I was on my trusty BlackBerry firing messages and e-mails off to both Rich and Marie, asking Rich to order books, and Marie for resources, all while running between planes in Philadelphia. This book would not exist without their assistance.

The faithful regulars of #prosapologian, my IRC channel, which functions a lot like my front room in many ways, had a very large part in getting this project done in a timely fashion. Folks like Micah provided tremendously important resources that helped me form the database from which the book arose. Any time I needed assistance, my ops and the regulars were happy to assist. Folks like justrozie and buzz were always willing to help in a moment's notice, and Jeff Downs, as always, was most helpful. One afternoon MarieP, crewbear and mutato were all transcribing video clips at the same time. MarieP, DeoVolente, and bluewoad all ransacked libraries for me, sending me pdf scans of obscure sources, or in one case, over-nighting an entire book. And as the chapters began to appear, MarieP (Marie Peterson) and Flamey (Carrie Gambill) took on the duties of proofing and editing, with some later assistance at the end of the project from mutato and bluewoad. To all those who helped, named or not, I say a heart-felt "thank you."

I dedicate this book fittingly to my daughter, Summer Marie White. May the Lord bless and keep you, protect you, lift you up, and keep you focused upon what really matters in this world. Keep your eyes upon the risen Savior and the eternity over which He is lord!

Table of Contents

Toronto

"This is the beginning, not the end." Simcha Jacobovici, *The Lost Tomb of Jesus: A Critical Look*

I was in the office early on a Saturday morning because I couldn't keep dates straight and had showed up at a friend's house to help him move a week early. So, not wanting to waste an early Saturday morning, I was in the office working away when a visitor joined our chat channel. He quickly dropped a URL in channel and asked if anyone had seen it. It was an announcement about an upcoming press conference featuring James Cameron and Simcha Jacobovici. When I first scanned the URL, I asked some questions in the channel about the nature of "proof" and the like, but over the next few hours I began to see a few more items appearing on the web providing tantalizing claims but precious few details. But what caught my attention early on was the conjunction of claims regarding DNA, statistics, and a wide range of high-level scholarship. I took this upcoming film seriously, spending a number of hours looking into everything I could find early on.

The first thought I had centered on the use of "DNA evidence." Having completed a major in biology in college which included a great deal of emphasis upon genetics, I knew enough to realize that there could be no standard by which to identify Jesus' DNA, hence, there had to be some other kind of application being made. But I likewise knew that when DNA evidence is presented in our modern culture, which finds in "the facts of science" its final authority, even in religious realms, many would find this to be unquestionable and "final" in all things. The old "science vs. religion" canard would raise its head once again. But beyond this, to speak of DNA meant that there had to be physical remains to examine. Was this a claim to have found the very bones of Jesus? The only possible conclusion one could arrive at was that this film was pronouncing the end of the Christian faith through a denial of the physical resurrection. How else could it be?

On that first day, as the news began to slowly surface in the media and on the Internet, I began to consider the need for a sober examination of its claims. Even if it ended up being a sensationalistic, conspiracy-driven piece similar to what is seen almost every year in the months and weeks before Easter, I knew it would require a sober response on the part of Christians who recognize 1) that the resurrection is the heart of their faith and therefore cannot be compromised while still calling the faith "true," and 2) that even bad arguments take on a life of their own and find a way of refashioning themselves over and over again. Any Christian who would profess his or her faith in the resurrection would, in all likelihood, have to be familiar with the outlines of this presentation, even if it turned out to be less than compelling or scholarly.

As an apologist, a writer, a professor, an elder in the church, I long to see believers equipped to do the task of ministry. But we live in a society trained, from infancy, to disbelieve. The Christian worldview has been utterly overthrown, not only in the society as a whole, but sadly in a large portion of that which calls itself the "Church." For many complex reasons[1] the front door of the church has been of little use in keeping the influence of a very anti-biblical, anti-Christian way of thinking out of the church. As a result, many who have been introduced to the faith in a context where the full spectrum of biblical truth is not presented are in little position to engage the strongest challenges of the opponents of Christianity today. An inconsistent theology often leads to an inability to defend the faith. These believers, insofar as a work of grace has been done in their hearts, will persevere in the faith, but without discernment and knowledge they will be crippled in their ability to give witness to the risen Christ who lives through them.

As I write, many are dismissing the story as a tempest in a teapot, another of the many failed attempts to attack the resurrection of Christ. But I must confess an uneasy concern over how this is being handled on all sides. Yes, secular scholars are dismissing the film for the obvious reason that it is based not upon bad scholarship, per se, but upon no scholarship at all. As we will note, the producers decided to skip the

---

[1] For more insight into some of the reasons, see my work, *Pulpit Crimes* (Solid Ground Christian Books, 2006).

process of doing serious scholarship, by-passing the very voices now being raised in opposition and, as a result, should not be surprised at the dismissive attitude of the academy that they have encountered. It almost seems like they saw it coming, as the book contains an undercurrent of criticism of standard academic procedures. And yes, Christians in general are laughing it off as well. But I am concerned about the grounds upon which many believers are dismissing the story. Very few know anything about *The Acts of Philip* or mitochondrial DNA test limitations, for example. Few could tell you that there is more than one Joses in the New Testament. Even fewer are dismissing the story because of a deep knowledge of the backgrounds of the New Testament itself, its history, its location in the geopolitical spectrum of the ancient world. No, it is being dismissed for all the wrong reasons. Instead of growing, learning, being prepared for the next onslaught (and there will be more), most are, I fear, dismissing the story on the basis of simple complacency: "Our experts say they are wrong, that's all I need to know." An opportunity to grow and to glorify God may well be missed for many.

At the same time, the book and film, with the accompanying website, are attracting the attention of many skeptics who find the idea of "scientific evidence" that the resurrection never took place most appealing. Attacks like this often take years, sometimes decades, to come to the fore. The core of *The Da Vinci Code* had been around for decades before Dan Brown sculpted it into a form that could produce hundreds of millions of dollars and finally attract enough attention to call for its full evaluation and refutation. This work is far more significant in its claims and its promoters far more savvy with the media.

Attacks upon the heart of the Christian faith are normative in Western culture today. It goes without saying that if any kind of film had been produced that had the same level of fundamental denial of Islamic belief that is inherent in the Jacobovici/Cameron work, a worldwide furor would have developed that would have made the Swedish cartoons saga of 2006 look like a garden party. But when the central affirmation of the Christian faith is attacked using highly questionable argumentation and data, no one has to worry about bombs going off or people dying in the streets. And evidently, because of that, Christianity seems to be "fair game."

It is painfully clear that those involved in the production of the film and book, while repeatedly disavowing religious interest, do, in fact, have worldview motivations. That is, the bias that I document on their part, the "spin" they place on the facts, the important pieces of information they somehow forget to mention, all point to a much less noble purpose. And with the launch of their very slick website[2] promoting the book and the DVD of the film, "the gloves have come off," and the press is on to promote worldwide the idea that Jesus Christ did not rise physically from the dead. One might excuse Jacobovici for being ignorant of Christian belief, but James Tabor well knows what he is promoting. There is no way to spin this film and book as anything other than what it is: a bold assertion that the central affirmation of Christianity is pure fiction.

The kind of radical skepticism demonstrated by the Jacobovici team is rampant in Western culture today. The media is far more interested in hearing what the Jesus Seminar has to say than to report on the verification of old truths believed by Christians for centuries. Men and women firmly committed to their rejection of the Christian faith will redefine the very parameters of scholarship just to make sure that the faith is marginalized, put in the worst possible light. When scholars speak, they assure us that whatever the situation, whatever the Bible teaches, or what Christians have believed, cannot possibly be the truth. This is simply a given for the skeptical academy of our day. This is where many find themselves today, in the skeptical climate of Toronto, and the faithful attitude of the disciples in Emmaus seems difficult to understand.

Why the Rush?

This book was written in the space of about seventeen days. I have written lengthy books in the space of months before, but only once have I written a book in a shorter space of time, and that one was not on a topic requiring documentation and research. So why the rush?

While there will be fuller, more extensive works produced in the months and years ahead, the fact is that this book and film were thrust upon the public in a media circus, precluding any kind of meaningful response at the time of their release. Because they have avoided the canons of solid scholarship, they have skipped past the "vetting" of their arguments, jumped directly to their conclusions, and presented them in a visually-oriented fashion specifically designed to arouse emotion, not sound and logical thinking. They have focused upon areas of scholarship that either demand great respect on the part of most people (DNA studies) or are far beyond the knowledge of the majority of people (Mid-East archaeology, ossuaries, probability statistics). As a

---

[2] http://www.jesusfamilytomb.com/

result, many desire to "hear the other side," and I have done my best to provide that response as quickly as time would possibly allow. Without a response, a terribly twisted, grossly inaccurate denial of the truth of the Christian faith will stand unchallenged until lengthier, fuller responses can be offered.

Another reason for the speed of this reply goes to my work as a Christian apologist. Many of the areas touched upon in the Talpiot story are common areas of interest in my work. Gnostic texts are an everyday "weapon" used against the Christian faith, for example. Canon issues, allegations of corruption, etc., are everyday fare for those seeking to defend the claims of Jesus Christ. So there were only a few areas that required immediate and new study on my part. For example, though I had seen *The Acts of Philip* in passing, I had never encountered an entire argument based upon its text. But my library, which is quite unusual in what it contains, gave me the opportunity to dig into its teachings and structure far more quickly than your average scholar.

It is my hope that this response, provided as quickly as time could possibly allow, will be an encouragement to the people of God who trust in the risen Christ. For those who have been troubled by the half-truths and spin of this attack upon the faith, it is my hope that seeing the whole story will allow them to more fully appreciate the truth. And for those who are considering the claims of Christ, it is my desire that this work, and those that will follow, will direct them to the Christ whose tomb remains empty to this day.

Why It Really Matters

> Now I make known to you, brethren, the gospel which I preached to you, which also you received, in which also you stand, [2] by which also you are saved, if you hold fast the word which I preached to you, unless you believed in vain. [3] For I delivered to you as of first importance what I also received, that Christ died for our sins according to the Scriptures, [4] and that He was buried, and that He was raised on the third day according to the Scriptures, [5] and that He appeared to Cephas, then to the twelve. [6] After that He appeared to more than five hundred brethren at one time, most of whom remain until now, but some have fallen asleep; [7] then He appeared to James, then to all the apostles; [8] and last of all, as to one untimely born, He appeared to me also. (1 Corinthians 15:1-8)

This is one of the earliest recorded traditions of the Christian faith. The epistle was written in the sixth decade of the first century, but it contains a tradition, passed on to Paul by the first generation of Jesus' followers, that goes directly to the words of Jesus himself barely twenty years earlier. There is only one step here from the original followers of Jesus to Paul.[3] The heart of the Christian faith is expressed in this primitive

---

[3] Contrast this tremendously early documentation that comes from first-hand sources, including eyewitnesses, as the origination of the tradition, which was publicly proclaimed during the time period when eyewitnesses could confirm, or deny, the events, with the wildly disconnected ahistorical fiction of *The Acts of Philip* from a vegetarian sect in Asia minor over three hundred years removed from these events! And yet it is to *The Acts of Philip* that the promoters of the tomb story turn for their foundation!

summary of the gospel: Jesus died for our sins, He was buried, and he rose again from the dead, and was seen by many witnesses. There is no question what "resurrection" means to Paul. It is not, in fact, some kind of spiritual reappearance. It is not people simply remembering Jesus. Given the Jewish context of the first century, resurrection means what it says: that which died coming to life again.[4] Physical resurrection. Jesus showed his disciples the marks of his crucifixion in his body. He had died, and he was alive again. This is the message of the Christian faith, the very message denied by *The Lost Tomb of Jesus.*

That same apostle Paul continued:

> [13] But if there is no resurrection of the dead, not even Christ has been raised; [14] and if Christ has not been raised, then our preaching is vain, your faith also is vain. [15] Moreover we are even found *to be* false witnesses of God, because we testified against God that He raised Christ, whom He did not raise, if in fact the dead are not raised. [16] For if the dead are not raised, not even Christ has been raised; [17] and if Christ has not been raised, your faith is worthless; you are still in your sins. [18] Then those also who have fallen asleep in Christ have perished. [19] If we have hoped in Christ in this life only, we are of all men most to be pitied. (1 Corinthians 15:13-19)

A Christianity without a risen Christ is unthinkable. A person who would deny himself and take up his cross for a Savior who did not rise from the dead is "of all men most to be pitied." In fact, as Paul says, if Jacobovici, Pellegrino, Tabor, and Cameron are right, Christians are guilty of having lied about God for two thousand years. And while they tracked down a few folks who claim to be Christians who do not believe in the resurrection, the fact is that every creed of every branch of the historic Christian faith, from the earliest days to today, all affirm an unquestionable belief in the resurrection of Jesus Christ from the dead. If there were bones to be tested by DNA, there was no resurrection, hence, no Christian faith.

---

[4] See the Appendix, "On the Resurrection," as well as the relevant portions of N.T. Wright, *The Resurrection of the Son of God* (Minneapolis: Fortress Press, 2003) on the lexicographical meaning and contextual usage of "resurrection" in the New Testament.

When Paul preached the message of Christ to the Greek philosophers at the Areopagus in Athens, he made an assertion that is very relevant to our inquiry regarding the resurrection:

> [30] "Therefore having overlooked the times of ignorance, God is now declaring to men that all *people* everywhere should repent, [31] because He has fixed a day in which He will judge the world in righteousness through a Man whom He has appointed, having furnished proof to all men by raising Him from the dead." [32] Now when they heard of the resurrection of the dead, some *began* to sneer, but others said, "We shall hear you again concerning this." (Acts 17:30-32)

This clearly demonstrates the meaning of "rising from the dead" in Paul's teaching. The Greeks, being dualists, found the idea of the physical body rising from the dead absurd because they viewed the spirit as good and that which is physical to be a burden, a prison, the locus of evil. To be freed from the physical body was salvation itself, so when Paul speaks of resurrection, the Greeks begin to mock.

But notice as well that the resurrection is, according to the Christian scriptures, God's proof of a coming righteous judgment. There is no Christian message left without an empty tomb. An ossuary filled with the bones of Jesus of Nazareth is the end of the Christian faith, and those who first proclaimed his resurrection would agree. There is simply no way to spin "He is not here, he is risen!" (Luke 24:6) into "He is not here. We moved him to another tomb, and his body is decomposing as we speak!"

The Lost Tomb Spin

> According to Christian faith, Jesus then ascended to heaven. In theory, the ascension could have been spiritual, leaving his body behind. In fact, those who take a strictly historical approach to the gospels would expect to find Jesus' remains in his family tomb.[5]

Personally, I would appreciate it if *The Discovery Channel* would actually consult orthodox, historic Christians to help define what "Christian faith" actually believes. They interviewed John Dominic Crossan, the

---

[5] *The Lost Tomb of Jesus*, Discovery Channel.

co-founder of *The Jesus Seminar.* I have debated Dr. Crossan, and will gladly confess that he is one of the nicest men I have ever met. But I am sure Dr. Crossan will not be surprised when I say that he is surely not representative of historic and believing Christianity. This is probably why he phrased his response as he did. Dr. Crossan does not believe in classical theism; he does not believe in an afterlife, let alone the physical resurrection of Jesus Christ.[6] So going to him to try to hide the fact that your film is a simple denial of the truthfulness of the Christian faith is significantly less than truthful. The same is true of the book's citation of a letter from a "Father Mervyn Fernando, Subhodi Institute, Sri Lanka." Any person who pretends to represent historic and biblical Christianity who denies the physical resurrection of Jesus Christ simply does not speak the truth. The clarity of the historic record is beyond question.

James Tabor, himself a former member of the Worldwide Church of God, tips his hand as to his views of Christian faith:

> When he's first buried it is in a temporary tomb. And later, unless he somehow magically disappears, and goes to heaven, which is the position of Christian faith, but if you're going to be historical and realistic, he'd be put in a permanent place, a permanent place of burial as a good Jew. Well, you have to have a family tomb...[7]

Please note the assertions of this scholar, which are central to the defense and presentation of the *Lost Tomb of Jesus* story. As a naturalistic materialist, Tabor likens the resurrection to "magically disappearing." Of course, nothing disappeared, the body rose to life, and he well knows this is the historic Christian faith, which he rejects. Notice that he contrasts Christian faith to that which is "historic and realistic." The reader needs to understand the central role of presuppositions in one's worldview. Tabor finds the resurrection unrealistic because his worldview does not have a category for it. Of course, it is ironic to see Dr. Tabor so confident in identifying the historic Gospels, which he knows are far more relevant to the first century than something as ahistorical as *The Acts of Philip*, taking this position. But what is more, this is the same scholar who has a picture of himself kneeling next to another supposed burial site of Jesus, this time in Galilee, in his book,

---

[6] See my debates with Dr. Crossan in DVD and mp3 format at www.aomin.org.
[7] *The Lost Tomb of Jesus*, Discovery Channel.

The Jesus Dynasty.[8] However, if you read the text, you discover that the "tradition" supporting this "tomb" comes from a "revered 16th-century Kabbalistic Rabbi Isaac ben Luria." *Sixteenth century?* The Gospels from the first century are to be dismissed as "magical" while a Kabbalistic Rabbi from the sixteenth century is to be trusted? Yet this is the face of so much of popular "scholarship" today.

> "The Lost Tomb Of Jesus" does not challenge the fact of the Resurrection. It does, however, ask viewers to consider the possibility that it occurred from another tomb.
> The writer of the Gospel of Matthew (28:12-15) addresses a rumor that was circulating in Jerusalem at the time of the Crucifixion, a rumor that we suggest can be taken for the truth. The rumor was that the disciples came by night to remove Jesus' body from the tomb of Joseph of Arimathea, a temporary tomb close enough to bury Jesus before sundown on the Sabbath. They would have moved Jesus to safeguard his remains from desecrators.
> His followers then would have taken Jesus to a permanent tomb, a family tomb.
> Theologically speaking, even if Jesus were moved from one tomb to another, this does not negate the possibility that he was resurrected from this second tomb. Our documentary does not address the issue of whether or not the Resurrection took place, and how. Belief in the Resurrection is based not on which tomb Jesus was buried in, but on alleged sightings of Jesus that occurred after his burial as documented in the Gospels.[9]

This is the "disclaimer" posted at the official website representing the book and the film. It partakes of the consistent error of redefining "resurrection" in light of selected individuals rather than the stated beliefs of Christian churches themselves. In any case, the website, and hence, by extension, the authors, are avoiding the reality of their claims. If there were bones in an ossuary till March of 1980 that belonged to Jesus of Nazareth, *there can be no resurrection.* It should be obvious to anyone that the term "resurrection" is to be defined, not on the basis of those who deny the faith or those who oppose the faith (like the Gnostics), but upon Christian use down through the centuries in light of

---

[8] James Tabor, *The Jesus Dynasty* (New York: Simon and Schuster, 2006), 239.
[9] http://www.jesusfamilytomb.com/movie_overview/disclaimer.html

the Scriptures themselves. But this the film and book refuse to allow, creating the odd situation where the promoters of the tomb theory can both deny the faith, and say they are not denying the faith, all at the same time. This may allow them to appear "politically correct," but personally, I would prefer a straight up and honest denial of the faith to the current "we will deny the central core of your faith but will redefine your faith so that we can say otherwise" approach.

> "Well," I said, "maybe. Maybe not. People who believe in a physical Resurrection would not be affected by the discovery of a Jesus bone box. In the Gnostic Gospels, Jesus appears before the apostles as a sort of holy ghost—here again, gone again. And he continues manifesting in this way for almost two years after the Crucifixion. In the four Gospels, Jesus only sometimes has a physical form—as when Doubting Thomas Didymos touches the five wounds only minutes after Jesus enters the room, spiritlike, through shut doors (see John 20:26–29). The author of Luke wrote almost apologetically, acknowledging at the start that all of this sounds strange but that this is how it appears to have happened. Read your Luke and John and you'll see what I mean. These people believed in a Resurrection that at times seemed to have been more or less physical, and at other times seemed entirely spiritual. [10]

I confess it is a bit frustrating to read this kind of material. Simcha Jacobovici candidly admitted in the book, "I'm an Orthodox Jew who grew up in a secular home and is better versed in Marxism than rabbinics."[11] Even if he had been familiar with rabbinics, that would hardly have put him in a position to make the kinds of pronouncements he does about the New Testament and Christian faith. When challenged, he consistently disavows expertise in theology, which is quite proper for him to do. However, if he disavows the ability to make pronouncements in the area, *why does he do so with regularity, as he does here?* None of those involved with the production of this tomb theory are professing Christians today, and the continual effort to avoid facing the reality of their claims is difficult to accept with equanimity. Saying people who believe in the resurrection would not be impacted by Jesus not rising from the dead physically is simply false. That is not a

---

[10] *TJFT*, 71-72.
[11] *TJFT*, 136.

resurrection. Calling the Gnostics as witnesses may impress those unfamiliar with history, but anyone familiar with the opposition to the faith posed by the Gnostics, and how the New Testament warns of their errors, will hardly find such a citation relevant. But it does show how willing Jacobovici and his fellows are to abandon the context of the New Testament *and* the Talpiot tomb (which are one and the same) to find support for their theories.

The authors then start sounding like secular Jehovah's Witnesses,[12] providing surface-level, a-contextual interpretations of the very text they elsewhere dismiss as self-contradictory and without historical merit! The authors of the texts cited all concluded that Jesus had risen from the dead physically, so why an attempt is made to spin even the text of the Christian Scriptures is hard to say (let alone believe). And it is offensive for a non-believer who is busy attacking the very heart of the Christian faith to flippantly mishandle and misrepresent the facts of the situation, such as in the above reference to Luke "apologetically acknowledging" that this all sounds "strange." Such a statement is either purposely false or intentionally misleading. Luke began his gospel quite clearly:

> Inasmuch as many have undertaken to compile an account of the things accomplished among us, 2 just as they were handed down to us by those who from the beginning were eyewitnesses and servants of the word, 3 it seemed fitting for me as well, having investigated everything carefully from the beginning, to write *it* out for you in consecutive order, most excellent Theophilus; 4 so that you may know the exact truth about the things you have been taught. (Luke 1:1-4)

These are the words of a man quite concerned about truth and the fact that what he is relating took place in history. He is indeed writing apologetically, but in the classical sense of the word, not in the sense used in the tomb book. He is not "uneasy" about what he is presenting at all. Instead, look at what he claims. He has compiled, from various sources, this account of things "accomplished among us," not things imagined or made up. These accounts were handed down not just to him as an individual, but to an entire community, spread across a wide geographical space. They came from those who had been *eyewitnesses*

---

[12] The Watchtower Bible and Tract Society denies the bodily resurrection of Christ, among other central Christian doctrines.

"from the beginning" (not mystics from the sixteenth century or vegetarian ascetics from the fourth). Luke boldly claims to have investigated his account "carefully from the beginning" so that he could write it out in an organized, understandable fashion. The result is that Theophilus, to whom he writes, might know not a myth or a legend or a muddled, confused message, but "the exact truth about the things you have been taught." Why would our authors even bother to make such a statement about Luke when the refutation of their misrepresentation is so easily obtained by doing what they suggest, reading Luke?

> "In any event, even a physical Resurrection doesn't depend on the fact that the first tomb was empty. It depends on Jesus's appearances among the disciples. A Christian believer can believe that Jesus was removed from the first tomb, traditionally identified with the tomb under the Holy Sepulchre in Jerusalem, and laid in a second tomb. With respect to his Ascension to heaven, the New Testament also does not tell us that its chroniclers believed that Jesus, when he ascended, needed to take his entire body with him. So if you believe in a physical Ascension, the ossuary is a problem. But if you believe in a spiritual one, it becomes an object of veneration."[13]

The Christian theologian and exegete must once again ask that those who are busily profiting from their denial of his faith stop playing games with his sacred texts. If there were bones left mouldering in an ossuary for around 1950 years or so, there was no resurrection, and there was no ascension. Period. It is a shift of meaning without merit to attempt to protect a "spiritual resurrection" while sacrificing a much less central "ascension" concept. All of this involves the most gratuitous misreading of the texts, all in an attempt to avoid saying "Christianity is bogus, always has been, and now, always will be." But I would say to our theorists, "We are accustomed to the attacks of those who deny the faith, so don't worry about that. Just state your position clearly and let us engage it on the level of truth." It would be a pleasure to debate these theorists in scholarly, academic debate, with both sides getting equal time, but it is that very platform of debate and examination that they by-passed by rushing their conclusions into the public realm in the first place.

---

[13] *TJFT*, 70-71.

It is interesting that Matthew records a contemporary tradition that shows how the authorities worried that Jesus's body would be taken by his disciples. They had gone underground, so to speak, and were not to be seen during the Crucifixion. But it was expected that they would now come and move the body. It is not odd that the authorities would have set "a watch" to secure the body of a man they perceived as a revolutionary leader, the "King of the Jews"; it is odd, however, that they would have secured the tomb by "sealing the stone." Tombs were sealed at the time of burial so as to prevent the body from being dragged away by animals. This mistake in the text is a clue that the writer of Matthew was not familiar with the mechanics of secondary burial. He probably added this scene as a way to refute a rumor that Jesus's body was taken by his disciples.[14]

It is interesting indeed that the film begins by rehabilitating the very first attack upon the Christian faith, honestly reported by Matthew himself, and that within the first minute of its opening scene. But even a cursory examination of the text once again shows us how far from a fair and truthful reading our tomb theorists are. Matthew does tell us that the Jewish leadership was concerned about the security of the tomb, but why? Evidently, our authors do not believe the majority of their audience will ever pick up a Bible to find out for themselves:

> [62] Now on the next day, the day after the preparation, the chief priests and the Pharisees gathered together with Pilate, [63] and said, "Sir, we remember that when He was still alive that deceiver said, 'After three days I *am to* rise again.' [64] "Therefore, give orders for the grave to be made secure until the third day, otherwise His disciples may come and steal Him away and say to the people, 'He has risen from the dead,' and the last deception will be worse than the first." [65] Pilate said to them, "You have a guard; go, make it *as* secure as you know how." [66] And they went and made the grave secure, and along with the guard they set a seal on the stone. (Matthew 27:62-66)

So why did the Jewish leaders go to Pilate? Because they, unlike our modern theorists, understood Jesus' claim. They knew that "to rise from the dead" was not a reference to some spiritual appearing to his

---

[14] *TJFT*, 72.

disciples after his death. They knew what "resurrection" meant. And so they were looking for Roman intervention and security. The seal is not, as supposed by our authors, the standard sealing of the stone in Jewish burial. This was a Roman seal, the breaking of which would carry the death penalty itself, protected by Roman soldiers. To read the above citation, alleging error on Matthew's part, when the error is so clearly on the part of those who refuse to allow Matthew to speak in context, or to take into consideration the rest of the New Testament evidence, is not only evidence of the shallow nature of the argumentation of the tomb theorists, but it is once again downright offensive to the Christian faith. If you are going to deny the faith, do so openly and honestly. But please, do not insult the text, the authors, and those of us who have studied their writings in faith, by misrepresenting them in such a shallow manner.

> There is another clue in the text as to what might have happened that "next day," the day of the Sabbath. Obviously, "the chief priests and Pharisees" hadn't posted a guard yet. The tomb was accessible. They had assumed that Jesus's disciples would not move the body on the Sabbath since among Pharisees that would have been regarded as a desecration of the holy day. They assumed that the disciples would wait until sunset— that is, until after the end of the Sabbath—and "come by night." They may have assumed wrong. Several times in the Gospels, Jesus's disciples appear to be more lenient with regard to Sabbath law than the Pharisees and Jesus himself (see Matthew 12:1–21 for one example). It's entirely possible—using the Gospels' own timeline—that the disciples came "by day," *during* the Sabbath. If they did, they could have easily moved the body. In fact, by being positioned to act, they could have waited until sunset in the tomb and then moved the body immediately *after* sunset, but *before* the guard had been posted. So it's entirely possible that Jesus's body ended up in a family tomb. If there was such a tomb, what would it look like to modern archaeologists?[15]

Once again our conspiracy theorists ignore the very text they are pretending to explain. When they write that it is "entirely possible," please realize that what they actually mean is, "If we assume the Gospel

---

15 *TJFT*, 73.

writers to be inveterate liars who foisted a fraud upon the entire world, then we can take snippets of what they wrote and spin them into an alternative theory, while rejecting their own testimony that they did not, in fact, take the body of Jesus." The text not only denies their conclusions, but affirms that when the women came (including Mary Magdalene), they brought with them the very materials one uses to prepare a body for final burial. If they had moved the body, why go through this charade? Once again we find our theorists mocking the text, misrepresenting what it says, and accusing the disciples of falsehood, all on the basis of what? What historical evidence do they provide? As we will see in the following chapters, the double standards used by them in choosing what they will accept as historical and what they will reject are simply astounding.

The *Discovery Channel* provided some interviews with Jacobovici and Cameron on their website. Jacobovici at one point observes:

> It's not about an Egyptian mummy. It's about Jesus of Nazareth. We're talking about people's fundamental beliefs and we try to be very respectful to those beliefs. What does it mean theologically if it is the bone box of Jesus? What does it mean? Well, you know we talked to theologians and they said - Christian theologians - and they said "It doesn't affect the resurrection at all. He could have risen from this tomb. He could have risen from that tomb." Does it affect the ascension? Well, if you believe that Jesus took his body to heaven, it does. But if you believe in a spiritual ascension, it doesn't. So we actually were kind of very respectful. We're not out there to prove or disprove anything.[16]

If there was not such a consistent pattern of spin/partial truths/suppression of facts contrary to the thesis on the part of Jacobovici, Pellegrino, Tabor, and Cameron in the book and the film, one would be more than justified in granting to Jacobovici the waiver of culpability he seeks for himself in these words. But there is just too much evidence to the contrary. As a believing Christian who has fully examined the "evidence" put forth in the light of twenty-five years of theological, historical, linguistic, and apologetic study, I do not believe *The Lost Tomb of Jesus* showed even a modicum of respect for the Christian faith. The makers of the film sought out the most unusual, the

---

[16] Simcha Jacobovici, *Discovery Channel Interview.*

most far-fetched, to represent the "norm" of my faith. No effort was made on their part to actually obtain testimony from those who would have serious objections to lodge against their views. The fact is, they *are* out to prove something (their theory), and any inconvenient facts that got in their way were simply thrust aside. I will document this particularly with regard to their historical sources, their use of the statements of scholars, etc., in the following chapters.

Finally I take note of the statements of the biggest name associated with the film, Oscar-winning director James Cameron.

> When I first heard the story that these guys had some pretty credible evidence that they had essentially found the tomb of Jesus and the remains of Jesus' family, I was intrigued by that because, even though I am not particularly religious myself, the idea that one of the most important human beings that had ever walked the face of the earth, there was now tangible historical evidence of his existence, which did not exist previously, had been found, you know, I wanted to be involved in the film project that would result from that.[17]

We should seriously consider the possibility that Mr. Cameron has truly never been evangelized so as to realize that the story he was so excited about involved the complete negation of the claims of "one of the most important human beings that had ever walked the face of the earth." Not knowing anything about the gentleman, I can only interact with what he has said, and as I will provide a full chapter of interaction with his claims later in the book, I will not engage that subject at this point. I cite these words only to demonstrate that from this perspective, Jesus can be viewed as "important" even if the central thrust of his message is eviscerated. Yet Mr. Cameron shows sufficient knowledge to realize that the thesis of the film and book is a bit more detrimental to the Christian faith than he may wish to admit:

> Well, I think it's fairly obvious to any Christian that finding the physical corporeal remains of Jesus is a big deal, certainly if you're a Roman Catholic, because of the belief in the physical resurrection. This film doesn't really attempt to deal with

---

[17] James Cameron, *Discovery Channel Interview.*

theological matters. We leave that to other people to discuss, who are more knowledgeable and an expert in that area.[18]

It is not only Roman Catholics who believe in the physical resurrection of Jesus Christ, of course. Catholics, Protestants, and Orthodox, all believe in the physical resurrection of Christ. To say that the film does not attempt to deal with theological matters is like saying ESPN does its best to avoid talking about sports. The entirety of the film is theological. Only a viewpoint that says that theology and faith are devoid of contact with history could substantiate such an assertion, and, of course, that is the very kind of "theology" belonging to those cited in the film. But historic Christianity knows nothing of a Christ who did not live in history and a faith that is not grounded firmly in reality itself.

And that is why it matters. The Christian faith proclaims boldly and loudly that God has not only created this world, but he has entered it personally in Jesus Christ. As the God-man, Christ humbled himself, took on human form, and lived and ministered in the first decades of the first century. He was truly man, and he was truly God. He ministered the word of life to those with ears to hear, and central to his message was the *necessity* of the cross. He went to Jerusalem purposefully, fully aware of what would happen. He gave his life voluntarily for a purpose, and, as he had prophesied, he rose again the third day from the tomb. He did not just move from one tomb to another, he rose from the dead, and his victory over death is what gives his followers their hope that through him, they too will conquer death. So nothing less than the very message of hope that is the Christian faith is at stake here. An ossuary containing the bones of Jesus means there is no resurrection, there is no hope. But, is that what they have found? The answer is a resounding "no." And to that issue we now turn.

---

[18] Ibid.

The Argument

It is my assumption that most of those reading this work have either seen the documentary *The Lost Tomb of Jesus*, read the book *The Jesus Family Tomb*, or both, but I recognize that some will read this work without having accessed these materials. So, while I cannot repeat the entirety of the presentation in the work, I do need to outline it, even for those who have seen the film or read the book. The main reason for this flows from one of the primary criticisms of the work itself: it presents its conclusions in the context of scientific investigation and scholarship; yet it does not present its arguments in a scholarly fashion. Simcha Jacobovici, Charles Pellegrino, James Tabor, and James Cameron chose to by-pass the normative channels of scholarship, which would have involved the presentation of each step in their argument in the context of professional journals and at professional meetings. Instead, they went straight to the final conclusion stage, by-passed the critical examination of their story, and presented it to the public. As a result, even the book skips from topic to topic, contains very little in the way of substantive, scholarly documentation, and leaves much to be desired for the person who truly wishes to take up the authors' challenge to examine and test their hypothesis. This was one of my earliest criticisms of the work, and it has been echoed by others. Jodi Magness of the *Archaeological Institute of America* has written:

> First let me point out that by making this announcement in the popular media, Jacobovici, Cameron, and the others involved have chosen to circumvent the usual academic process. Archaeology is a scientific discipline. New discoveries and interpretations typically are presented in scientific venues such as professional meetings or are published in peer-reviewed

journals, where they can be considered and discussed by other specialists. By first making the announcement in the popular media, those involved have precluded legitimate and vital academic discourse. This is because it is impossible to explain the many flaws of their claim in a one-minute segment on TV or the radio, or in two or three sentences in the newspaper, as I have been asked to do repeatedly since the announcement was made. The history and archaeology of Jerusalem in the first century are far too complex to be boiled down to a short sound bite, yet that is precisely what has happened here. This is a travesty to professional archaeologists and scholars of early Judaism and Christianity, and it is a disservice to the public.[19]

We will have reason, many times, to ponder the by-passing of the normative canons of scholarly inquiry on the part of Jacobovici and company, especially when we encounter the consistent suppression of counter-evidence found in the very same sources being cited in the film and the book. The repetitive nature of this problem must be taken into consideration when examining the over-all intentions of the writers.

The Talpiot Tomb

This is not a new story, though for most, it is quite novel. On March 28, 1980, while beginning work on the construction of apartment complexes in the Talpiot suburb of Jerusalem, southwest of the main city, a bulldozer broke into the fore portion of an ancient tomb from the first century, A.D. More of the details will be chronicled below as presented in *The Jesus Family Tomb* (hereafter *TJFT*). For now, suffice it to say that ten ossuaries (limestone bone-boxes) were removed by archaeologists from the tomb, six of them bearing inscriptions. The bones were removed as per an agreement with the "ultra-orthodox" Jews and given a Jewish burial elsewhere, away from ravaging, earth-moving equipment. The ossuaries were stored away by the Israel Antiquities Authority[20] (IAA) after being cataloged and recorded. In 1996, one of the archaeologists involved in the initial excavation, Amos Kloner, published an article[21] describing the tomb and its contents. The same year, a BBC news team bumped into the ossuaries and, noting the

---

[19] http://www.archaeological.org/webinfo.php?page=10408
[20] At the time called the Department of Antiquities.
[21] Amos Kloner. "A Tomb with Inscribed Ossuaries in the East Talpiot." *Atiquot* 29 (1996): 15-22.

inscriptions, published an article foreshadowing the events of Spring, 2007. But without the combined resources and drive of Simcha Jacobovici and James Cameron, the story fizzled very quickly.

What resurrected, literally, a story that had been known, at least in some circles, for almost three decades? In a word, or more specifically, a name, Emmy award-winning journalist Simcha Jacobovici. Israeli-born, Canadian-raised Jacobovici is not only the star of the film, he is clearly the linchpin to the project. The book presents him as the one who "connected the dots" and brought together the group who made the book and film possible. And while he is quick to say he is not an archaeologist (though producing a series about himself called *The Naked Archaeologist*), not a theologian, not a DNA expert, not a statistician, etc., there is truly no question that all of the relevant materials—the book, the film, interviews on the Today Show, Larry King Live, etc.—all confirm that the final product seen on our television screens in early 2007 is his vision and encompasses his conclusions.

Jacobovici was drawn to the Talpiot tomb through the "James, Brother of Jesus" ossuary documentary he likewise worked on for the Discovery Channel. He describes the genesis of this project in a Discovery Channel interview posted at www.discoverychannel.com, contemporaneous with the release of the film. As we will see in the following chapter, this "discovery" by Jacobovici is the very heart of the entire theory propounded in the film and the book. Without it, the entirety of the argument collapses, which is why we will look so closely at it. Here is how he described it in the Discovery Channel interview:

> The key moment in the investigation was the identification of the second Mary ... So then the question becomes "Well, why didn't anybody pay real attention to this tomb?" And there were two things kind of going against this cluster of inscriptions. One was that they were supposedly common names. Jesus, Mary, Joseph. Common names. Finding them together doesn't mean anything. The second is the second Mary. The two Mary's in Jesus' life as everybody knows: one is his mother; you know the virgin Mary; and the other is Mary Magdalene. You know, post-DaVinci code everybody knows Mary Magdalene. Now had the second Mary said 'Mary Magdalene' then, you know, the world would have come grinding to a halt. But it didn't. It didn't say Mary Magdalene, so that was used... It said Mariamne, which is a Greek version

of the word Mary. And that was used as a way of dismissing... Well, that proves it. It's not the tomb of Jesus of Nazareth.

So I had to look first at that issue - the second Mary. And interestingly enough, I just... You know, I had never heard Mary Magdalene referred to as anything but Mary Magdalene. But when I researched into it, I realized that Mary Magdalene is not a name. It's a title. It's like Mary the New Yorker or Mary the Torontonian. It's Mary from the town of Magdala. So, well, if that's her title - if that's her nickname if you will, Mary the Magdalean – what's her name? Well you know I found out that scholars don't argue about that. Because of the Gnostic gospels, because of the *Acts of Phillip*—several ancient texts that have recently been discovered, the *Acts of Phillip* in the seventies. Scholars agree what Mary Magdalene's real name is, and her name is Mariamne. Greek Orthodox Church still calls her Mariamne—still celebrates Mary Magdalene. You know there's a day of celebrating Mary Magdalene as... by her name Mariamne - the Greek version of Mary.

And guess what? That is what it says on the ossuary—on the coffin—found next to Jesus, son of Joseph. So it's that moment that the light bulb went on. That the very thing that people were using to dismiss this tomb was the very thing that at the end of the day would prove that ... or that would make the argument that this tomb may indeed be the tomb of Jesus of Nazareth.[22]

On the *Today Show* of Monday, February 26, 2007, Jacobovici and James Cameron appeared in an interview with Meredith Vieira promoting their film and book. At one point, Cameron seeks to explain why the original archaeologists did not see the Talpiot tomb as significant in 1980:

To be fair to them, there was a critical piece of information they didn't have available. They said, "Oh, well there's a second Mary here. You know, Mariamne is a diminutive of Mariam, which is Mary. But they didn't have the information from the Acts of Philip which *definitely*[23] identifies Mary Magdalene as

---

[22] Simcha Jacobovici, *Discovery Channel Interview.*
[23] Cameron strongly emphasized this term.

Mariamne. If they'd had that information, they might have looked at the whole name cluster differently in 1980. Simcha found that information.

We will have occasion to interact with this claim in the next chapter (for now, I will simply say the *Acts of Philip* does not do any such thing, and, even if it did, such would carry the historical weight of the *National Inquirer* reporting that George Washington was a space alien). The point for now is that Simcha Jacobovici "discovered" that the *Acts of Philip* makes the connection between Mariamne and Mary Magdalene, and this was what allowed them to "connect the dots" and see that the Jesus family tomb had been discovered in 1980. This was the "turning point," and it led, eventually, to the testing of mitochondrial DNA, the construction of a statistical argument, and even the rediscovery of the Talpiot tomb buried in the gardens of the apartment complex.

We can turn to the Jacobovici/Pellegrino text[24] to fill out most of the rest of the story. The book begins by literally raising the very same story the early church reported in the first century:

> 11 Now while they were on their way, some of the guard came into the city and reported to the chief priests all that had happened. 12 And when they had assembled with the elders and consulted together, they gave a large sum of money to the soldiers, 13 and said, "You are to say, 'His disciples came by night and stole Him away while we were asleep.' 14 "And if this should come to the governor's ears, we will win him over and keep you out of trouble." 15 And they took the money and did as they had been instructed; and this story was widely spread among the Jews, *and is* to this day. (Matthew 28:11-15)

Without coming right out and saying it, the film leaves us with no doubts as to the authors' view of the integrity of the apostles. Their entire presentation is based upon the removal of Jesus' body from the first tomb by the disciples. How this could have possibly happened, given the guard at the tomb, we will consider at a later point. But from the start it is self-evident that for the promoters of this theory, the integrity of the New Testament is a non-issue. It has no authority outside of the facts they choose to accept from it. Otherwise, they

---

[24] Simcha Jacobovici and Charles Pellegrino, *The Jesus Family Tomb: The Discovery, Investigation, and the Evidence that Could Change History* (Harper San Francisco, 2007).

dismiss its testimony, when it contradicts their theory, as later theology. Indeed, James Cameron, in his foreword to the book, boldly claimed:

> The Gospels as we know them today have been retranscribed and rewritten many times and translated from one language to another—from Aramaic to Greek to Coptic to Latin to various forms of English—with corresponding losses in nuanced meaning. They have been edited by Church fathers, centuries after the original words were spoken, to conform to their subsequent vision of orthodoxy.[25]

We will demonstrate the very basic error in Cameron's understanding at a later point, but for now we note the bias that lies upon the very surface of the key players in the promotion of the Jesus family tomb theory. The book goes on to assert:

> If the disciples took the body, there is only one thing they could have done with it. They would have reburied it.

> If Jesus was reburied, his family would have waited for his flesh to disappear and then stored his bones in an ossuary, sealed away forever deep in the recesses of his family tomb.[26]

There is no reason to dispute the idea that it was the original intention of those who placed Jesus in the tomb after His crucifixion to return, complete the burial process, and allow the body to decay for a year and then return and place the bones in an ossuary. This was indeed a common practice of the day. However, the assumption throughout the book that is never meaningfully substantiated is this: that Jesus' family would have had a tomb in a city other than their hometown. Who ever did that? It is Jesus of *Nazareth* not Jesus of *Jerusalem*. Jesus was a visitor to Jerusalem, like literally hundreds of thousands of others who would have been there over Passover. It would have been the normal plan to carry the ossuary back to Jesus' home in Galilee. The idea of a Jerusalem burial site for the entire family stretches scholarly credulity to the breaking point.

---

[25] *TJFT*, x.
[26] *TJFT*, 2-3.

In any case, once the book and film set up the scene, they move forward to 1980 and the discovery of the tomb. In describing it, they relate:

> In antiquity—clearly no one had entered this tomb recently—someone had removed the five seal stones that should normally have walled up the kokhim. Displacement of the seals and removal of the stones were sure signs that looters or vandals had entered the tomb at some point ahead of the entry of the red soil. And yet the ossuaries remained, in apt and self-contradictory fashion, with their lids undamaged and perfectly in place, as if the intruding looters or vandals had been interested in neither looting nor vandalism.[27]

The "red soil" to which they make reference is the *terra rosa* which later made its way into the tomb, climbing up to the level of the tops of the ossuaries. The fact that the tomb had been entered in antiquity, but long after its original construction, is extremely important. On any level, it raises questions concerning the validity of the find, the identity of those who got in, etc. This needs to be remembered, for it truly does not enter into the thinking of the authors of the theory presented in the film and the book. In any case, it is not mentioned in the book that Amos Kloner, in his 1996 article on the tomb,[28] estimated that there were *thirty-five* interments in the tomb, seventeen in the ossuaries, and eighteen outside. This would mean there were multiple people per ossuary. This too should be kept in mind.

One of the experts on the original excavation, now deceased, was Yosef Gat. We read in *TJFT*:

> Gat examined the workmanship on the two shelves and admired the attention to detail. "It's a good-sized tomb, carved with great care under the direction of someone not lacking funds," he observed. "Important people were buried here."[29]

This is an important point as well. This was not just a hole in a hillside. It took money, and therefore standing and influence in the Jewish

---

[27] *TJFT*, 9.
[28] Amos Kloner, "A Tomb with Inscribed Ossuaries in East Talpiyot, Jerusalem." Atiquot XXIX, 1996, 15-22.
[29] *TJFT*, 9.

community of Jerusalem, to construct it. And one thing that is quite certain from the most ancient records that actually derive from the Jewish context of Jerusalem is this: while a small number of influential men, like Joseph of Arimathea and Nicodemus, became followers of Christ, Jesus himself in no way had any standing in the city of Jerusalem proper. He did not live there, his family was not based there, and he was, from their perspective, an outcast. Surely there is no reason at all to think He ever had such a standing before the crucifixion, and there is far less reason to think he and his family would be welcome there afterward. This tomb was not hidden and hence would have been known to the Jewish leaders. This too becomes a major problem for our theorists. The book correctly observes:

> Also, by and large, ossuary use did not spread to the masses. Real estate in Jerusalem, then and now, is extremely expensive. Only the religious, political, and economic elite could afford family crypts or tombs in which to store the ossuaries. The poor were buried in the ground (either by simple placement into little niches cut into the local "chalk stone" or by burial in soft earth, far beyond the city walls). The people who could afford tombs or who had a religious reason for practicing this particular form of burial were placed in ossuaries.[30]

And a little later:

> After all, because of the existence of ossuaries, we have a veritable phonebook of Jerusalem's political, economic, and religious elite dating back to the time of Jesus.[31]

To demonstrate the initial element of the theory propounded in this book, our authors will have to explain how Jesus can be described as one of the "religious, political, and economic elite" of Jerusalem. This is a tall order, given the evidence that exists that he was not even a part of the Jerusalem community, but was clearly seen as an outsider, a Galilean, a second-class citizen at best, without connections to the Pharisees, Sadducees, and scribes, and, in fact, seen as their greatest critic.

The Talpiot tomb was unusual in that six of the ten ossuaries had inscriptions on them. This is unusual because, on average, only about

---

[30] *TJFT*, 27.
[31] *TJFT*, 28.

20% of the one thousand or so ossuaries thus far discovered bear inscriptions. So this was a high percentage for a single tomb.

The use of ossuaries is somewhat of an oddity in the first place. The practice flourished for only 80 to 100 years, from about 20 B.C. until the destruction of Jerusalem by Titus and the Roman legions in A.D. 70. It was popular only in Jerusalem, with others found in Jericho, and some in Galilee. But its locus was definitely Jerusalem. Ossuaries (less technically known as "bone boxes") were generally made out of limestone, some with, and some without, ornamental decoration.

As the archaeologists looked at the ossuaries being removed from the Talpiot tomb in March of 1980, they noticed very popular Jewish names. They found two forms of the name Mary, specifically, "Maria" and "Mariamne." They found a very nicely made ossuary with the name "Yudah bar Yeshua," Judah the son of Joshua or, in its more popular Western form, Jesus. A Matthew was found, and a Jose, the diminutive form of Joseph, again one of the most popular names in Jewish tombs of the first century. And finally, they found "Yeshua bar Yosef," Jesus, son of Joseph. And, once again, this did not cause the excavation to stop so that the world could be apprised of this monumental find, for Yeshua, we know today, is the sixth most popular name found in such tombs. The same name had been found on another ossuary in 1926, so this was not the first. In fact, in an article in *Biblical Archaeology Review*, it was estimated, based upon the current listing of names from ossuaries, writings, inscriptions, and the like, that during this time period in Jerusalem there would have been around 5,600 men named "Yeshua, son of Yosef," and at least twenty men named Yeshua son of Yosef with a brother named James![32] Of course, that is only looking at those

---

[32] Andre Lemaire, "Burial Box of James the Brother of Jesus" BAR 28:06 (Nov/Dec 2002). Biblical Archaeology Society:

> The names of James (Jacob), Joseph and Jesus were all fairly common among Jews at the turn of the era. Rahmani's catalogue of ossuaries in Israel lists 233 inscriptions. All three names are among those that appear the most frequently. Joseph is found 19 times, Jesus ten times and James/Jacob five times. Rachel Hachlili has studied names used at this time in all types of inscriptions. Joseph appeared in 14 percent, Jesus in 9 percent and James/Jacob in 2 percent of the cases.
>
> Based on these percentages, we can conclude that about 0.28 percent (a little more than a quarter of a percent) of the male population were named either "James/Jacob, son of Joseph" or "Joseph, son of James/Jacob." So about 0.14 percent were named "James/Jacob, son of Joseph." Of these people, how many would also have a brother "Jesus"? Assuming that each male had approximately two brothers, this would mean that about 18 percent

living in Jerusalem. Taking into consideration all of Judea and Galilee, the number would be greatly increased. And, of course, since Jesus did not live in Jerusalem, but in Galilee, that is the context that one would logically examine in reference to the probability of finding a "Jesus family tomb." Finally, there is another reason why at least those familiar with the New Testament would find the inscription "Yeshua bar Yosef" less than shocking: none of those close to Jesus ever called him by this name. Only his enemies used similar terminology, not his friends. So if this is the Jesus family tomb, why use language that would have been at home in the mouths of his enemies,-rather than his friends?

It is interesting to note the words of Simcha Jacobovici at this point:

> Along with most of the world, I did not know what an ossuary was, and I certainly didn't know that the Christian Gospels claim that Jesus had siblings. I now realize that the general ignorance concerning ossuaries, and also concerning Jesus's family, is precisely what has allowed the story of the discovery of the Jesus family tomb to linger in the shadows for nearly thirty years.[33]

It is unsettling to note that Mr. Jacobovici came to this story without even the most surface level knowledge of the New Testament, and that, in a very short time, he came to the conclusion that the same collection of documents is untrustworthy (except in the few details he chooses to fit into his theories). Despite how often he seeks to qualify his assertions, it is clear that he believes this is in fact the Jesus family tomb, and that the entire Christian faith and its central affirmation regarding Christ's resurrection is false. The possibility that it is Mr. Jacobovici's starting presuppositions that are in error, and that this gives rise to an entire book full of false connections and erroneous conclusions, does not seem to factor into his thinking. Jacobovici truly seems to believe Jesus lived in Jerusalem:

---

of the men named "James/Jacob, son of Joseph" had a brother named Jesus. Accordingly, over two generations, 0.05 percent of the population would likely be called "Jacob son of Joseph brother of Jesus."

The estimated population of Jerusalem at this time was about 80,000, which means that about 40,000 of the people were male. In Jerusalem during the two generations before 70 C.E., there were therefore probably about 20 people who could be called "James/Jacob son of Joseph brother of Jesus." It is, however, impossible to estimate how many of these 20 people were buried in ossuaries and how many of these ossuaries would be inscribed.

[33] *TJFT*, 26.

> And historically speaking, the most famous family engaged in secondary burial and living in Jerusalem in the first century was the family of Jesus.[34]

Evidently he truly believes, upon some unknown basis, that Jesus of Nazareth became Jesus of Jerusalem, though he never even attempts to make the argument from any source at all. But despite this self-professed ignorance of the New Testament, its contents, history, transmission, textual manuscript tradition, etc., both Jacobovici and Pellegrino are more than happy to import the most radical viewpoints into their work, resulting in a tremendously skewed foundation that gives rise to their theory. They will take as given facts names, for example, like "Mary Magdalene," and locations, like Jerusalem, but, when it suits their goals, ignore the very same texts and their testimony to historical realities. This is done repeatedly, and often just in passing, without any references offered, no arguments given, no recognition of the mountain of Christian scholarship they are by-passing in their haste to judgment. For example, Jacobovici writes:

> The people who touched Jesus, talked with him, broke bread with him, and believed in his Messiahship were all Jewish. But after his Crucifixion, a Jew named Saul, who became the apostle Paul, rose to lead a Gentile following that threatened to overwhelm the original group.[35]

Yes, the original followers of Jesus, with few exceptions, were Jews. So was Paul. But then we have inserted, without comment or explanation, an entire anti-Pauline assumption that ignores the testimony of the New Testament itself, let alone Paul's writings. This is part of the attempt to throw a very positive light upon the Ebionites, or as the book prefers to refer to them, the "Judeo-Christians." The theory is that there are a large number of tombs in and around Jerusalem that are actually Christian, in the sense of Judeo-Christian. They make reference to those Ebionites who rejected the deity of Christ and maintained distinctive Jewish religious practices, and connect these "original followers" of Jesus to the Jerusalem area so as to provide for some kind of basis of Christian burial in Jerusalem. This is their means

---

[34] *Ibid.*
[35] *TJFT*, 35.

of criticizing the Israeli Antiquities Authority, Amos Kloner, and the great body of modern archaeologists, who, they say, simply "assume" that all the burials in Jerusalem are Jewish. Much time and effort is spent on this theoretical argument, as we will see later. They make mention of the work of Professor Sukenik who likewise believes there are many Judeo-Christian burial sites in Jerusalem. Jacobovici writes, "But think about it: if Sukenik was right and you could locate early Judeo-Christian tombs, why not the tomb of the family of Jesus?"[36] Note the connection they are seeking to forge. For now, we note that after dismissing, without so much as a meaningful argument, the entirety of Christian orthodoxy, all of the Pauline contributions to the New Testament, etc., Jacobovici claims,

> The Church fathers, the men who shaped Christianity, either ignored the Ebionites and Nazarenes or dealt with them in various polemics against heretics—in fact, these writings are often our only record of some of these groups. After all, there was no point in overly stressing their existence; given that these emphasized the historical Jesus over the theological one, doing so might lead to embarrassing questions such as, "If Mary was a virgin, how is it that Jesus had four brothers and two sisters?" That problem was dealt with, incidentally, by turning his siblings into half-brothers and half-sisters, or into cousins. But other questions were harder to deal with, such as, "If Jesus and his followers kept the Sabbath, followed kosher laws, and practiced circumcision, why don't Christians?" Of course, theological answers can always be formulated, but it was best to ignore the people who once walked with Jesus. Simply put, by continuing to be practicing Jews, the Judeo-Christians were an embarrassment to the early Church.[37]

Since it is clear that Jewish Christians, like the Apostles, believed in the deity of Christ and the virgin birth, yes, the Ebionites were rejected, just as the "false brothers" of Galatians 2:4 were rejected for their false teachings on the nature of the gospel of Christ. It is not that they were an "embarrassment," they were amongst those who denied the most fundamental truths of the Christian faith. The Ebionites were not emphasizing a "historical" Jesus over a theological one at all: that is

---

Jacobovici's bias showing through.   He assumes the Jesus of history
could not be the Jesus of the Christian faith, but he never once attempts
to engage in the kind of argumentation one would have to present to
make such an argument.   He may well not even know that there is
sound, consistent Christian scholarship behind a belief in a divine and
risen Savior. But that seems a bit unlikely.

The Names of Talpiot

The key to the argument is found in the names inscribed upon the
six ossuaries in the Talpiot tomb.   The most famous, of course, is
Yeshua bar Yosef, Jesus, son of Joseph. Then we have Maria, the
"Latinized" form of the very common Mariam, the most common
woman's name in the entire period.   There is a second Mary in the
double-name "Mariame kai Mara." Here the controversy rages, for the
film and book are all based upon reading this inscription as Mariamne o
Mara, "Mariamne the Master." But Stephen Pfann of the University of
the Holy Land in Jerusalem has strongly contradicted this reading in a
paper published shortly after the book and film came out.[38] Pfann's
argumentation is compelling. As we will see in the next chapter, the
identification of this particular ossuary, based upon the assumption 1)
that there is only one person in the ossuary (contra the published
documentation from the original archaeologists and the best reading of
the inscription), 2) that Mariamne is the name of the person in the
ossuary, not Mariame and Mara, and 3) that fictional works written by
ascetic groups in Asia minor three centuries later are determinative of
how to read inscriptions in ossuaries from the first century in Jerusalem,
is the means of determining that this is actually the ossuary of Mary
Magdalene, who then becomes married to Jesus. As utterly far-fetched
as that sounds, that is exactly what we will see is the argument, and it is
the focal point of the entire theory. Simcha Jacobovici provides the
following notation he wrote down as the light began to dawn on him
about what the Talpiot tomb actually represents:

> d. "Mariamne also known as Mara." Greek inscription.
> According to prominent academics, such as professors François
> Bovon and Karen King of Harvard, this is Mary Magdalene's
> real name. The professors don't seem to know this ossuary

---

[38] http://www.uhl.ac/MariameAndMartha/

exists. If she is Mary Magdalene, what's she doing in Jesus's "family" tomb? Were they married?![39]

Likewise in the tomb is Mattia, a form of Matthew, a name not associated with Jesus' family at all, though the authors go back into Mary's family line and try to make a connection in this manner. Of course, to archaeologists simply examining this tomb, it is clearly multi-generational, spanning at least three, possibly four generations. It was clearly in use longer than the time period in which Jesus visited Jerusalem during his ministry. In any case, with as many as 35 people found in the tomb between the ground and the ossuaries, one could have a wide variety of relationships in the family represented, from cousins to nephews to uncles. What is more, given the fact that the true owners of the tomb clearly had connections and money, they may have had servants, which, given the history of the area, could explain the fact that Mariamenou Mara is written not in Hebrew but in Greek lettering. She very well could have been a servant to his important family. All of these rational, obvious considerations are passed off in the rush to turn this into the Jesus Family Tomb.

Also found is Jose. Evidently, Jacobovici had not begun reading the New Testament at a certain point in his studies, for he relates informing James Tabor about his theories, and then ends an entire chapter with a build up to the following from Tabor:

> "In the Gospel of Mark," Tabor whispered as he leaned forward. "'Yosa' or Jose in English, *Joses* in Greek—is explicitly mentioned as one of Jesus' four brothers."[40]

If a drum roll could be inserted into the written text, it would surely be at this point. Ironically, Tabor is right, but, as with so much in this book, only partially right. Yes, Joses is the name given to Joseph, one of Jesus' brothers, in Mark (did Peter know Joses well enough to use the less formal term, and this comes through in Mark?). But what is not mentioned in the film or in the book is that this is not the only Joses in the New Testament. There is another Joses, who likewise had a mother named Mary, and a brother named James ("the less"), Mark 15:40. And in the Byzantine manuscript family, in Acts 4:36, Barnabas is given the name Joses as well. When the book and film focus in upon how rare

---

[39] *TJFT,* 61-62.
[40] *TJFT,* 65.

and unusual it is to find this form, it would be materially relevant to note these other instances in the New Testament, but no mention is made. And once again, when you find a name on an ossuary that has never been found before, keep in mind that 10% of all names on ossuaries have only been found once. The sample size, again, is so small that no meaningful conclusions can be drawn from that fact alone.

Finally we come to the last name, Yudah bar Yeshua, Judah, son of Jesus. Again, nothing unusual to find three generations in a single tomb (Yosef, Yeshua, Yudah), and Joseph, Joshua/Jesus, and Judah are hardly shockingly uncommon names in first century Palestine. But, of course, if you have a "plot" to create, a story to spin, and you want to prove this is the Jesus Family Tomb, this becomes an important piece of your puzzle:

> "Judah, son of Jesus." The most explosive ossuary in the tomb. In some ways, more explosive than Jesus. If "Mariamne" was Jesus's wife, is this their son? It's the smallest ossuary in the tomb. "Judah" died as a kid? But the Gospels never mention a son? Could "Judah" be the enigmatic "Beloved Disciple" mentioned in the Gospel of John?[41]

Jacobovici's willingness to make the "beloved disciple" connection to the gospel of John may be one of the reasons many scholars who would be otherwise sympathetic to anything opposed to Christianity have, thus far, kept their distance. This kind of speculation is so far outside the bounds of "journalism" and "reporting facts" that it betrays the true intentions of the parties involved.

Spinning the Web

So now we have the foundation of the story. How to prove this is the Jesus Family Tomb? Jacobovici, Pellegrino and Cameron bring together three main threads of argumentation: the Mariamne/Mary Magdalene connection is the heart. Everything else depends upon it. Without it, there is no family tomb, no conspiracies to be woven on the screen before the awed eyes of millions. So much effort is put into turning Mariamne into Mary Magdalene. And so we will invest just as much effort in examining the effort.

Next, the authors invoke the sacred name of modern secular culture, the scientific Holy Grail itself, DNA. One can almost hear

---

[41] *TJFT*, 62.

Grissom saying, "We have DNA. The facts don't lie." All of the early press releases focused upon DNA analysis. And surely we cannot dismiss the weight DNA carries in scientific investigation, even in the ancient context. But what can DNA analysis tell us about these ossuaries? What are its limitations? And what hidden presuppositions did the authors bring to their examination, if any? The authors claim that the DNA analysis done by Dr. Carney Matheson of Lakehead University in Thunder Bay, Ontario, lays the foundation of their theory that Jesus and Mary Magdalene were married because the DNA analysis shows that the human "debris" (small bone fragments embedded in the bottoms of the ossuaries) found in the Yeshua ossuary and the Mariamne ossuary do not "match." Or, to use Jacobovici's words in the press conference announcing their "discovery," "The forensic archaeologist concluded that they must be husband and wife."

But to close the case, another approach was needed. In the first days after the opening salvo of their presentation, Jacobovici repeatedly retreated to the "statistical analysis," the third major plank in the argument. Based upon the information given to Andrey Feuerverger of the University of Toronto, a statistician, it was calculated that, in the most conservative form, there was a 600 to 1 chance that the "name cluster" of Jesus, Mary, Mary Magdalene (based upon the Mariamne connection), and Joses would all be found in the same tomb together. When the James ossuary is added to the scheme, the chances jump to 30,000 to one, and again, that is conservatively speaking. It could be in the many millions to one. This has been the oft-repeated argument in the book, film, and on the part of the purveyors of this theory since they made their announcement. "What is the chance," they will say, "that there just happened to be a man named Jesus, whose father was named Joseph, who had two women in his life named Mary, and a brother named Joses, other than the Jesus of Nazareth we know of from the Bible?" This has been their "trump card," and given the lack of general discernment and knowledge of statistical probabilities arguments in the general population, we will have to invest some effort in explaining the argument. For the moment, suffice it to say that the entire probability expression is assuming the one thing that is actually under dispute: it begins with the assumption that the Jesus family tomb exists amongst the tombs discovered and excavated in Jerusalem. But that's the whole point: there is no reason to believe Jesus would have had a family tomb in Jerusalem to begin with.

Now, if the book and film had ended here, I think a few more scholars would have signed on for the ride. But it didn't, and though the book goes farther into what can only be called esoteric speculation than the film does, both make an obvious pitch for what I call the "Da Vinci Code crowd," those folks looking for some off-the-wall theory to believe in regarding Jesus.

In the film, time is wasted speculating on how Judah, the son, in the film, of Jesus and Mary Magdalene, might be the "beloved disciple" mentioned in the Gospel of John. The film discusses how dangerous it would be for Judah to be associated with Jesus, so secrecy was a must. He is shown being protected from the sight of a Roman soldier by his mother. And then he and Mary Magdalene are shown at the foot of the cross, and the film speculates that Jesus' words, understood by many centuries of Christians as having been spoken to Mary, Jesus' mother, and John, the beloved disciple, were actually addressed to his family. Of course, with Roman soldiers standing around, that would have been a pretty dangerous thing to do, but at this point, we are really not dealing with anything meaningful in the historical sense in the speculations being thrown out by the film and the book.

But while the film stops here, the book plows ahead with abandon. It actually promotes the idea that Judah, the son of Jesus, was the author of the second-century Gospel of Thomas. Now, given that the best date for the Gospel of Thomas is around A.D. 165, and the Talpiot tomb would have been sealed and closed by about A.D. 65 at the latest, it would be very hard for Judah to write a Gnostic gospel down in Egypt somewhere a century after he was buried, but trivial historical problems like this simply cannot get in the way of a good story!

But missing from the film completely was the best impersonation of Dan Brown's *The Da Vinci Code* found in the book. You simply cannot have a conspiracy theory about something in Jerusalem without including the Knights Templar! And so an entire section is included in the book speculating about the shape of the decoration over the Talpiot tomb and how possibly the Knights Templar had come to Jerusalem and had encountered the Judeo-Christians (the Ebionites) and had forced them to reveal the secret of the Jesus family tomb! So they were the ones who got in, realized what it was, and held its secret over the Pope's head, which is why they gathered so much power and influence in such a short period of time. Of course, as we all know, the Pope took care of them eventually, but it must have been this secret that gave them so much power! As I said, this may well be the reason why some who would otherwise be very sympathetic to the over-all thrust of the film have been slow to commit to its ideas.

This brings me to a final thought before we move into the specific refutation of the claims of the book. For many, in light of known historical facts, the entire premise of the book and film has already been refuted. In the Ted Koppel inquiry aired after the film on the Discovery Channel on March 4, 2007, two scholars dismissed the primary argumentation as naïve and without merit. Others clearly agree. So why press on with this book? Two reasons amongst many can be cited. First, there is a long line of exploded myths running back into recent history regarding Jesus and his life and teachings, but those myths keep coming back to life in new forms, only to be exploded again. This is just the first "incarnation" of this story. Someone may well take some of its main elements, switch them around, add a few new twists, and try all over again. The foundations of the argument need to be fully examined, and refuted, right from the start. Secondly, I predict that someone is right now rummaging through 1980s vintage burial records, looking for the bones that came from this tomb. Others are trying to find a way into the other tomb just 20 meters from the Talpiot tomb. Still others may be trying to scour through the remaining ossuaries, looking for DNA. There may well be more to come in this story, so we dare not rest complacently upon a surface level examination of its claims.

The Heart of the Story: Mary Magdalene MIA

When *The Family Tomb of Jesus* story began circulating I did all I could to analyze the argument and determine what made this new denial of the resurrection of Christ different from what had come before. The first reports were so vague and sensationalistic it was impossible to focus in upon the heart of the argument. In fact, it was not until the book was released a few days before the film aired that the real nature of the argument could be examined. It only took a single reading to realize that the DNA argumentation was peripheral and dependent upon another assumption. Likewise, the statistical evidence was based upon certain assumptions, certain presuppositions, and was therefore peripheral to the real argument.

The *Discovery Channel* provided a series of on-camera interviews with both Simcha Jacobovici and James Cameron immediately after the airing of the film. In the interview with Jacobovici the centrality of one particular "fact" comes to light. I quote him in full:

> The key moment in the investigation was the identification of the second Mary ... So then the question becomes "Well, why didn't anybody pay real attention to this tomb?" And there were two things kind of going against this cluster of inscriptions. One was that they were supposedly common names. Jesus, Mary, Joseph. Common names. Finding them together doesn't mean anything. The second is the second Mary. The two Marys in Jesus' life, as everybody knows: one is his mother; you know the Virgin Mary; and the other is Mary Magdalene. You know, post-Da Vinci Code everybody knows Mary Magdalene. Now had the second Mary said 'Mary Magdalene' then, you know, the world would have come

grinding to a halt. But it didn't. It didn't say Mary Magdalene, so that was used... It said Mariamne, which is a Greek version of the word Mary. And that was used as a way of dismissing... Well, that proves it. It's not the tomb of Jesus of Nazareth.

So I had to look first at that issue - the second Mary. And interestingly enough, I just... You know, I had never heard Mary Magdalene referred to as anything but Mary Magdalene. But when I researched into it, I realized that Mary Magdalene is not a name. It's a title. It's like Mary the New Yorker or Mary the Torontonian. It's Mary from the town of Magdala. So, well, if that's her title - if that's her nickname if you will, Mary the Magdalean – what's her name? Well you know I found out that scholars don't argue about that. Because of the Gnostic gospels, because of the Acts of Phillip - several ancient texts that have recently been discovered, the *Acts of Philip* in the seventies. Scholars agree what Mary Magdalene's real name is, and her name is Mariamne. Greek Orthodox Church still calls her Mariamne - still celebrates Mary Magdalene. You know there's a day of celebrating Mary Magdalene as... by her name Mariamne - the Greek version of Mary.

And guess what? That is what it says on the ossuary - on the coffin - found next to Jesus, son of Joseph. So it's that moment that the light bulb went on. That the very thing that people were using to dismiss this tomb was the very thing that at the end of the day would prove that ... or that would make the argument that this tomb may indeed be the tomb of Jesus of Nazareth.[42]

When James Cameron joined Jacobovici on the *Today Show* to announce their "discovery," he likewise confirmed that the "Mariamne connection" is the very heart of this entire theory:

> To be fair to them, there was a critical piece of information they didn't have available. They said, "Oh, well there's a second Mary here. You know, Mariamne is a diminutive of Mariam, which is Mary. But they didn't have the information from the Acts of Philip which *definitely* identifies Mary Magdalene as Mariamne. If they'd had that information, they might have

---

[42] Simcha Jacobovici, *Discovery Channel Interview.*

looked at the whole name cluster differently in 1980. Simcha found that information.[43]

But it is not only in interviews that the centrality of the Mariamne ossuary has been emphasized:

> But other than the Jesus, son of Joseph ossuary, to use Feuerverger's term, the most "surprising" of all the ossuaries in the Talpiot tomb is the one inscribed "[the ossuary] of Mariamne also known as Mara." From the beginning, we focused on this particular ossuary because it seemed to be the key to the whole story. Everything depended on this unique artifact. Nonetheless, we did not learn its secrets right away. They were revealed slowly over time.[44]

"Everything depended on this unique artifact." This is quite true. The entire theory collapses without this keystone. But what exactly is being claimed? The argument is not overly involved, but it does involve some incredible leaps of logic, history, and science.

Let's summarize the argument:

- Talpiot ossuary 80-500 (Rahmani 701) bears the inscription "Mariamne, also known as Mara"
- The 4th century apocryphal work, *The Acts of Philip,* makes reference to a woman named Mariamne.
- *The Acts of Philip* identify Mariamne as Mary Magdalene.
- Therefore, Mary Magdalene is the Mariamne of Talpiot Ossuary 80-500.

Then, anticipating the discussion of the following chapters,

- Mary Magdalene is in the Talpiot tomb with Jesus, son of Joseph.
- Also in the tomb is Judah, son of Jesus.
- DNA analysis proves Mariamne is not related to Jesus by birth.
- Therefore, Jesus and Mary Magdalene were married, and Judah is their son.

---

[43] James Cameron on *The Today Show*, February 26, 2007.
[44] *TJFT*, 204.

This is the simplest way to summarize the argument. It likewise helps us to lay it out so that we can address each step of the argument and analyze the validity of the argument as a whole.

Here is an image of Talpiot ossuary 80-500 (Rahmani 701):

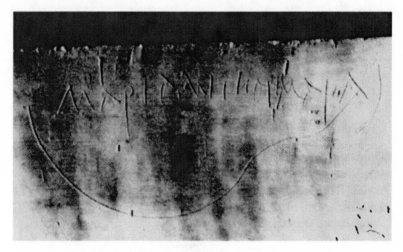

The inscription appears as follows:

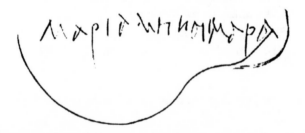

The consistent reading of this text given by the film and the book is "Mariamne, also known as Master." The specific spelling of the first name is very important in the argument, for it is the sole link to *The Acts of Philip*.

To see if this argument bears the weight placed upon it by our theorists, we need to ask the following questions:

- Does the inscription on the ossuary read "Mariamne, also known as the Master"?
- Does *The Acts of Philip* contain references to a Mariamne?
- If so, does *The Acts of Philip* identify Mariamne as Mary Magdalene?
- Should *The Acts of Philip* be used to determine identifications of first century inscriptions in tombs in Jerusalem? Is it relevant?

In my opinion, if the argument fails here, the rest of the entire film and book are left without any basis or foundation and, from the preceding citations from Jacobovici and Cameron, they would have to agree. I will address this issue in two parts. First, what does the inscription actually say? And second, is *The Acts of Philip* connection valid in any way? The second question may seem irrelevant after the first, but it also gives us a chance to shine the light on the kind of "scholarship" that is prevalent in Western media today. So let's begin with the inscription itself.

Mariame, Mariam, Mariamne, Martha, Master?

Let us look once again at the inscription as provided by Rahmani:

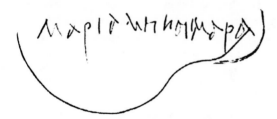

There is tremendous controversy over the actual reading of this inscription. It is obviously not done by a professional hand. Likewise, it is quite unusual for the obvious reason that it is not written in Hebrew, but in Greek. Though you would not know it by watching the film or reading the book, there is a tremendous amount of question as to the actual reading and interpretation of this inscription. In fact, the reading that is necessary for the theory to move to its next stage is one of the *less likely* readings. Let's start with the two most likely scenarios.

ΜΑΡΙΑΜΗ ΚΑΙ ΜΑΡΑ
Mariame kai Mara

First we will note the work of Stephen J. Pfann, Ph.D., of the University of the Holy Land in Jerusalem. In a paper[45] posted shortly after the release of the film, Pfann renders the inscription as shown above, "Mariame and Mara," or, in English, "Mary and Martha." He argues that the second portion of the inscription was written by a later hand at a later time. In other words, the original inscription was simply Mariame, and when Mara's bones were added, her name was added to the inscription in a different hand. One does note, even in the graphic provided here, that the "rho" (r) in Maria is formed quite differently than the one found in "Mara" at the end of the inscription. Pfann likewise provides references from other sources where the Greek word "kai" was written in the form found here. Pfann appears briefly in the film as an expert on ossuaries, so his expertise and his access to Jerusalem ossuaries, etc., cannot be questioned. This is surely one of the two most likely readings.

ΜΑΡΙΑΜ Η ΚΑΙ ΜΑΡΑ
Mariam e kai Mara

This is the reading suggested by Maurice Robinson of the Southeastern Baptist Theological Seminary. Robinson believes it is better to recognize a common form for "also known as" between the normative form of Mariam (found often in the New Testament) and the name Mara. Likewise, there are New Testament grounds for reading η και in this fashion. This reading then would be, "Mary, who is also known as Martha."

ΜΑΡΙΑΜΕΝΟΥ ΜΑΡΑ
Mariamenou Mara

This is the reading given originally by L.Y. Rahmani and Amos Kloner. The genitive construction "Mariamenou" could be interpreted as "Mary's Martha," possibly playing on the diminutive form of Martha, "Mary's little girl Martha." Mariamene is the Greek form of the Hebrew "Mariam," or simply, Mary. Given that this is in the genitive form, the nominative would be Mariamene, or, Mariamne.

---

[45] Stephan Pfann, "Mary Magdalene is Now Missing: A Corrected Reading of Rahmani Ossuary 701." http://www.uhl.ac/MariameAndMartha/

Now it should be painfully clear to the fair reader that our theorists begin their journey on very shaky ground. Two of the three readings, the two most likely readings, strip them of their first and most necessary assertion, "Mariamne." Now, you would never know of these other readings if you simply watched the film or read the book. The third reading is taken for granted. But if we were to use statistics (and who could argue against that?), we would have to point out that at best their position is based upon a reading that is only 1/3 possible. In reality, it is probably only about a 20% chance that that reading is the correct one. So a long line of tenuous argumentation begins with a first step that admits of far better possibilities that would contradict it. Are we really ready to overthrow the entire testimony of the apostles, the credibility of the Gospels, on an argument that starts like this? One truly wonders.

Mary Magdalene: A Brief Introduction

Before we can analyze the claims made by Jacobovici and his team regarding the Mariamne/Mary Magdalene connection, we need to introduce those not familiar with her to the biblical presentation of this follower of Jesus Christ. You surely would not get a meaningful introduction from such popular fictional works as *The Da Vinci Code*.

Like many others in the narratives of the Gospels, Mary Magdalene appears as a follower of the Messiah. But we are told very little about her. In three of the Gospels, Matthew, Mark, and John, she appears only at the end of the story of the life of Christ.[46] She is present at the crucifixion as well as at the resurrection. Christ appears to her as one of the first to see him alive:

> Now on the first *day* of the week Mary Magdalene came early to the tomb, while it was still dark, and saw the stone *already* taken away from the tomb. 2 So she ran and came to Simon Peter and to the other disciple whom Jesus loved, and said to them, "They have taken away the Lord out of the tomb, and we do not know where they have laid Him."... 11 But Mary was standing outside the tomb weeping; and so, as she wept, she stooped and looked into the tomb; 12 and she saw two angels in white sitting, one at the head and one at the feet, where the body of Jesus had been lying. 13 And they said to her, "Woman, why are you weeping?" She said to them,

---

[46] Matthew 27:56, 61, 28:1; Mark 15:40, 16:1; John 19:25, 20:1, 18.

"Because they have taken away my Lord, and I do not know where they have laid Him." 14 When she had said this, she turned around and saw Jesus standing *there*, and did not know that it was Jesus. 15 Jesus said to her, "Woman, why are you weeping? Whom are you seeking?" Supposing Him to be the gardener, she said to Him, "Sir, if you have carried Him away, tell me where you have laid Him, and I will take Him away." 16 Jesus said to her, "Mary!" She turned and said to Him in Hebrew, "Rabboni!" (which, means Teacher). 17 Jesus said to her, "Stop clinging to Me, for I have not yet ascended to the Father; but go to My brethren and say to them, 'I ascend to My Father and your Father, and My God and your God.'" 18 Mary Magdalene came, announcing to the disciples, "I have seen the Lord," and *that* He had said these things to her. (John 20:1-2, 11-18).

Surely Mary's faithfulness as a disciple is rewarded with this encounter with the risen Christ even before he appears to his disciples. Her presence at the crucifixion, while the others had fled, is likewise a testimony to her dedication and strength of character. But nothing at all is suggested of anything similar to the theory put forth by Jacobovici.

The one Gospel writer that speaks of Mary earlier in his work is Luke. Luke has a special interest in the women of faith who were part of Jesus' ministry. We read in Luke 8:1-3,

> **Luke 8:1-3** Soon afterwards, He *began* going around from one city and village to another, proclaiming and preaching the kingdom of God. The twelve were with Him, 2 and *also* some women who had been healed of evil spirits and sicknesses: Mary who was called Magdalene, from whom seven demons had gone out, 3 and Joanna the wife of Chuza, Herod's steward, and Susanna, and many others who were contributing to their support out of their private means.

Luke likewise gives us personal insights into the very thoughts of Mary, Jesus' mother, so it is obvious that he had direct contact with her, and quite probably with others as he worked to collect their testimonies regarding the sayings, teachings, and life of Jesus. And it is for this reason that we should look closely at what Luke says here. Jacobovici tells us that Mary Magdalene's "real name" was Mariamne. Luke would have met the woman, unlike the anonymous author(s) of *The Acts of*

Philip over three hundred years later! Luke is known for his peculiar accuracy in the use of specific terms to properly designate government officials, for example, in chronicling Paul's journeys through Asia Minor. He has a way with names. If her "real" name was Mariamne, Luke would have known this. Instead, he says, "Mary who was called Magdalene." In the original language of this book, she was Μαρία ἡ καλουμένη Μαγδαληνη, "Mary, the one called, known as, Magdalene." He uses Maria, not Mariamne, and indicates that Magdalene was part and parcel of her normative appellation. It is interesting to note that the next time he mentions her, on the morning of the resurrection, he writes, "Now they were Mary Magdalene and Joanna and Mary the *mother* of James; also the other women with them were telling these things to the apostles" (Luke 24:10). At first glance this may not seem at all relevant. However, it should be noted that when the other writers refer to Mary Magdalene, they normally do so in this form: Μαριὰμ ἡ Μαγδαληνη (John 20:18) or Μαρία ἡ Μαγδαληνη (Mariam or Maria). The name comes first, followed by the reference to "Magdalene." But Luke had emphasized that term earlier, so notice how he refers to her in Luke 24:10: ἡ Μαγδαληνὴ Μαρία. Was this a stylistic change only, just a reflection of Luke's more formal style? Or was this the emphasis that flowed from his personal knowledge and interest in these faithful female disciples? We cannot be sure, but one thing is for certain: there is not a sliver of evidence for the "Mariamne" connection to be found in the only documents actually written in the first century by those most closely associated with Jesus and his ministry.

The Acts of Philip

If you are like 99.95% of the human population, you had never heard of *The Acts of Philip* before encountering the tomb story. Even as one who works in the field of apologetics, I had only marginal familiarity with the work. *The Gospel of Philip* is much better known. The work exists in only a handful of manuscripts, the earliest of which comes a full one thousand years after the original work was written. The text is horrifically corrupted, as we will see. If you only read the tomb book, or watched the film, you would scarcely learn anything *factual* about *The Acts of Philip*. But you sure would end up thinking highly of it! In fact, you would probably have to conclude that *The Acts of Philip* is far more historically relevant to first century Judea and to the city of Jerusalem than any of the canonical Gospels, Matthew, Mark, Luke, or John. The book is quite willing to accuse the Gospels of falsehood and misreporting, and to assert that they were later edited and changed, etc.

But *The Acts of Philip* is never subjected to this kind of criticism. Of course, the means by which our theorists came across this vital source of information might cause a few people to wonder a bit at just how discerning they have been. Jacobovici relates:

> "Well," I said, "in the Talpiot tomb they found ten ossuaries, six with inscriptions. The inscribed ones include a "Matthew," a "Joseph," two "Marys," and a "Jesus, son of Joseph."
>
> Ron raised an eyebrow. "And no one noticed?"
>
> "Well," I retorted, "one Mary was called Maria, which merits attention, but the other was called. . ."
>
> "Magdalene?" he interrupted, laughing.
>
> "No, Mariamne," I said.
>
> "Never heard of her. Too bad," he chuckled, and got back to work.
>
> "Look into her," I said. "See if there's a connection between the names Mariamne and Magdalene."
>
> "Well," Ron smiled a toothless grin, "today we have the Internet. Why don't we look into it right now?" He googled "Mariamne" and then turned slightly pale. "Look, Simcha," Ron exclaimed. Over his shoulder I peered at the screen and the article his search had led him to. "According to modern scholarship," he read out loud, "Mary Magdalene's real name was Mariamne."[47]

While the Internet can surely be a wonderful source of useful information, we have all come to understand that there is a need for further inquiry before accepting everything we find listed in a Google search. What is more, the oft-repeated assertion that "Mary Magdalene's real name was Mariamne" is simply *wrong* on every level it can be, as we will see. Unfortunately, Jacobovici, Pellegrino, Tabor, etc., show not the slightest interest in exposing their key source, *The Acts of Philip*, to any scrutiny at all. Instead, they simply repeat the same mantra over and over again, referring to the work repeatedly, *but never once citing the text itself.* As we will see, there is a reason for this, and if you spent $25 on the book, you might not be happy with what you are about to discover.

---

[47] *TJFT*, 45.

But let's make sure we understand how fully invested in the historical accuracy and relevance of *The Acts of Philip* Jacobovici and his colleagues are. In the film, we have a full reenactment with the following offered by the narrator:

> The strong leadership displayed by Magdalene would have been regarded as suspect by an evolving male-dominated church. So from the second century when church fathers began suppressing dozens of early Christian writings, the church rejected two texts that held Mary Magdalene in highest regard, *The Gospel of Mary Magdalene*, and a text describing her brother's ministry, *The Acts of Philip*.[48]

In the images you see hooded monks reading, and then burning, pages of manuscripts. It is all very conspiratorial and said in all seriousness. Of course, to anyone even slightly familiar with church history, the entire assertion is tremendously humorous. The church of the second century was itself being "suppressed," and that savagely, by the might of the Roman Empire. *The Gospel of Mary Magdalene* may have been written during that century, if its earliest dating is accepted. But there is not a shred of evidence Mary Magdalene was Philip's brother, of course. And what is amazing is the statement that the church of the second century was suppressing *The Acts of Philip* since, *as the film itself goes on to assert*, it was written in the *fourth century*. Just how did the second-century church suppress a writing that would not appear until the fourth century? One can only speculate.

The film's presentation of *The Acts of Philip* goes to tremendous lengths. For example:

> However, in *The Acts of Philip*, written in the fourth century, the oldest known account of Mary Magdalene's travels, she does not die in France.

> Bovon: According to the Acts of Philip, at the end of the story, Mariamne is supposed to go home to Israel to the Jordan Valley and the author has an allusion to where she will die and be buried.

---

[48] *The Lost Tomb of Jesus*, Discovery Channel.

> *The Acts of Philip* clearly tells us that Mary Magdalene, Jesus'
> most trusted apostle, dies here, in Jerusalem.[49]

Notice the last claim made. Right after showing Francois Bovon, a
Harvard professor, the film pans across Jerusalem and claims *The Acts of
Philip* says Mary Magdalene would be buried in Jerusalem.

Bovon figures prominently in both the book and the film. He is
presented as the final authority on *The Acts of Philip*, and his authority is
invoked for the film's historical identification of Mary Magdalene in this
"historical" source. Francois Bovon is the Frothingham Professor of
the History of Religion at Harvard University. He is likewise one of
those who found the most complete manuscript of *The Acts of Philip* in
1974 in the library of Xenophontos Monastery on Mount Athos in
Greece. The manuscript he discovered was from the fourteenth
century. It differs in numerous aspects from the versions of the work
contained in less full manuscripts, and in particular, the main manuscript
from which the text had been known before his discovery, *Vaticanus
graecus 824*.[50] In reality, the text of this work is quite corrupt, with no
way to determine its original form, given that the time span between the
writing of the text and the first manuscript evidence is a full thousand
years. Of course, neither the film nor the book mentions anything
about this. The text of the book is assumed to be even more reliable
than that of the New Testament. There is, in fact, no comparison
between the rich manuscript tradition behind the New Testament and
The Acts of Philip. Every book of the New Testament has a hundred
times the manuscript evidence and textual purity.

With this background, let's document the claims of our Talpiot
theorists regarding *The Acts of Philip* and Francois Bovon. Then we will
look at the book itself, the community that produced it, and whether it
is actually relevant to the Talpiot tomb or not. We begin with these
claims:

> The Acts of Philip is an apocryphal New Testament text left out
> of the official canon. In the second century, "apocryphal"
> meant either "secret" or "rejected." The Acts of Philip was
> widely quoted by early Christian writers but was eventually lost

---

[49] *The Lost Tomb of Jesus*, Discovery Channel.
[50] Other manuscripts include *Parisinus graecus 881*, *Vaticanus graecus 866*,
Ambrosianus graecus 405, and *Atheniensis 346*.

save for a few fragments. In 1976[51] scholars François Bovon and Bertrand Bouvier were permitted to examine the contents of the library at the Xenophontos Monastery on Mount Athos. There, miraculously preserved, they discovered an almost complete fourteenth-century copy of the Acts of Philip transcribed from texts compiled perhaps a thousand years earlier.

In June 2000, Bovon and Bouvier published the first complete translation—into French—of the Mount Athos version of the Acts of Philip, with its identification of Mary Magdalene as "Mariamne," the sister of the apostle Philip. The Acts of Philip provides us with a much more complete version of Mary Magdalene than the Gospels.[52]

Note that the book claims the book contains an "identification of Mary Magdalene as 'Mariamne,' the sister of the apostle Philip." The authors truly believe that the stories included regarding Mary Magdalene in *The Acts of Philip* are historical in nature. Perhaps it is this naiveté, especially on the part of Jacobovici, which allowed him to so completely misunderstand the answers given to his questions by Bovon when they met at Harvard. The book reports Bovon saying to him:

"And she is a strong figure, Simcha—identical to the picture of Magdalene we receive from another ancient text, the Gnostic Gospel of Thomas. According to these scribes, Jesus seemed to empower women.[53]

This is where the "connection" comes in: Bovon says the Mariamne of the story of the *Acts* is "identical to the *picture* of Magdalene we receive from another ancient text, the Gnostic Gospel of Thomas." As Bovon has confirmed to me directly (citation provided below), he is speaking of *literary* not *historical* connections here. He is speaking of a genre of literature, far removed from the historical context of Jerusalem, and is commenting on parallels he sees between the person Mariamne in *The Acts of Philip* and the Mary Magdalene found in Gnostic sources from the second century. But so intent is Jacobovici to turn the Talpiot tomb

---

[51] The date is actually 1974.

[52] *TJFT*, 95-96.

[53] *TJFT*, 96.

into the end of the Christian faith that he misses the vital distinction. We continue:

> "This Mary Magdalene," Bovon told Simcha, "this Mary from the Acts of Philip, is clearly the equal of the other apostles—and, as depicted, is even more enlightened than Philip.[54]

Once again, this is said in the context of *literary parallels,* not history. He is speaking of characters that had meaning to a particular community, and we will see soon what concerns on their part gave rise to the fictional work that is *The Acts of Philip.*

> Bovon perceives a rather more mystical meaning, buried now in a church culture lost to antiquity. He observes that a very similar message is echoed in the final verses of the Gospel of Thomas, a message that a manly or womanly body is to be viewed as amounting to nothing more than an outward husk that "clothes" the spirit; all that really matters, in the final judgment, is the "spirit" that dwells within.[55]

The view of man and woman in Gnostic writings, which have influenced *The Acts of Philip,* is surely different than that of the Bible and the Christian faith in general. This makes these writings popular today with academics in particular who dislike the Christian faith, but it likewise gives the Gnostic writers from Nag Hammadi, and those influenced by them in later generations, a reason to create fictional characters who fit their polemic against the "established church."

> The matter of Mary Magdalene's status in the ministry and her conflict with Peter was addressed again in the Gospel of Mary Magdalene, discovered at Nag Hammadi, Egypt, in 1945.[56]

As interesting as the Gnostic texts are, it should be remembered that they are far removed from the historical setting of the events of Jesus' life and ministry. They come from a completely different worldview than what is found in Judaism and therefore in Christianity. They come from a century later, at the earliest, the best dating for such works as *The*

---

[54] *TJFT,* 97.
[55] *TJFT,* 98.
[56] Ibid.

Gospel of Thomas being around 165.[57] Their authors were, in many cases, purposefully seeking to contradict the very teachings we find in the New Testament. In fact, both John and Paul make reference to early Gnostic beliefs and warn the early Christian congregations against them.[58] These were not neutral authors, but they were instead seeking to overthrow the teachings of the very men who lived and walked with Jesus. As popular as it is to seek to rehabilitate these early enemies of the Christian faith, the fact is that they were just that: enemies to the movement Christ founded. Jacobovici continues:

> It seems that the Acts of Philip are a window on early Christian belief, and on the meaning of the IAA 80/500–509 inscriptions. "In this text," Bovon explained to Simcha, "Mariamne's group traveled through Syria, northward into the Greek-speaking world. And this apostle, Mariamne, is attested to in ancient Christianity as a Greek formulation for Mary Magdalene—and here, in the original Greek, in these Acts of Philip, we have, of course, been reading this very same name.[59]

Unfortunately, as you will notice, there are no closing quotes in this citation. It would be significant to know where Bovon's quote closes and Jacobovici's commentary begins, or if this is all Bovon. In any case, we will have opportunity to examine these "other references" to Mariamne below.

> "To be clear," said Bovon, "in the Acts of Philip the first Mary—Magdalene—is called Mariamne. The second Mary is also mentioned, but only once, in a speech about the birth of Jesus. And she is called—"

> "Maria," Simcha finished for him.

> "Maria," Bovon repeated.

---

[57] See Craig Evans, *Fabricating Jesus: How Modern Scholars Distort the Gospels* (Downer's Grove: IVP Books, 2006), 67-77.
[58] John's first Epistle is filled with anti-Gnostic and anti-Docetic teaching, and Paul uses many specific terms used in Gnostic doctrine in his letter to the church at Colossae as a means of teaching the congregation to avoid their errors.
[59] *TJFT*, 100.

> "And Mary Magdalene—" "Is clearly Mariamne," said Bovon.
> "So there is no confusion here between the two persons."[60]

Jacobovici is clearly taking Bovon to be referring to historical identifications, when Bovon is speaking of literary categories and parallels. Yes, the Encratite community of Asia Minor that produced the *Acts* knew enough to differentiate between Mary, the mother of Jesus, and Mariamne. But as we will see, this is hardly relevant to identifying inscriptions in first century Jewish tombs in Jerusalem.

> "In Israel. This, again, is somewhat different from the predominant tradition—which has her settling somewhere in the south of France. Yet, at the end of the Acts of Philip, Mariamne goes home to Israel, and that's where she would die and be buried. This is the earliest tradition."[61]

This is the final citation of Bovon, and again, especially in light of my correspondence with him, the phrase "earliest tradition" should not be confused with "earliest solid historical tradition" but "earliest literary speculative tradition." Pondering whether Mary Magdalene went to France or back to Israel, given the nature of these sources, is far beyond the historian's realm, for these works cannot seriously claim historical provenance. But Jacobovici is not interested in such fine distinctions, for he closes his section with these words:

> The Acts of Philip provided very important information to be weighed against the Talpiot tomb. First, it provided a name for the mother of Jesus: Maria, and one for Mary Magdalene: Mariamne; second, it provided a status for Mariamne—she was an apostle, a teacher, or, to use the Aramaic, a "Mara"; third, she moved in Greek circles; and fourth, her bones were buried in Israel.[62]

Please keep something in mind here: so far, you have not seen a single word of *The Acts of Philip* cited from Jacobovici and crew in support of their theory. Not a word. All you find is a brief citation from the book

---

[60] Ibid.
[61] *TJFT,* 102.
[62] Ibid.

in the reading of Bovon regarding Philip,[63] but nothing in support of the Mariamne/Mary Magdalene connection. Does that not seem strange? But there is a reason, as we shall see when we come to examine the text.

As the book begins to collect the various threads of its theory, the centrality of *The Acts of Philip* once again comes to the fore:

> James Tabor, using other ossuaries as precedents, pointed out that the "Mariamne" inscription should be read: "[the bones] of Mariamne also known as 'Mara.'" For our part, we learned that, independent of the Talpiot discovery, leading Mary Magdalene experts have concluded that the woman known in the Gospels as Mary Magdalene was actually called by the Greek version of her name: "Mariamme," [Mariamene, or Mariamne]. The information comes, in the first instance, from the Church father Origen, who calls Magdalene "Mariamme," and then from the writer Epiphanus and noncanonical texts such as the Pistis Sophia. But the clincher is the Acts of Philip.[64]

We are not told who these "leading Mary Magdalene" experts are, but we can guess, from other references, that Tabor is referring to Karen King and Francois Bovon. But let us examine closely the "proof" offered of this absolutely necessary element of the argument. We are told that Origen "calls Magdalene 'Mariamne.'" But we are not told when or in what context. This is the kind of sloppy argumentation that the process of scholarship would have cleared up.

The *Thesaurus Linguae Graece* is a massive collection of ancient Greek writings on CD-ROM. A quick scan of Origen's writings reveals a single reference in his large work *Contra Celsus*. Celsus was an early venomous critic of the Christian faith, and his writings are becoming more popular even today as anti-Christian sentiment becomes ever more popular. Origen, himself worthy of an entire book biographically speaking, was responding to Celsus' accusations regarding the multiplicity of "sects" claiming to be Christian.[65] He is writing in the early third century. Real scholarship would provide the citation and

---

[63] *TJFT*, 96.

[64] *TJFT*, 205.

[65] Ironically, I heard this very argument of Celsus' repeated by a member of the "Rational Response Squad" during the course of the writing of this book, proving once again that there is "nothing new under the sun" when it comes to those who attack the Christian faith.

allow the reader to evaluate the claim. Here is the English translation, with the Greek provided in the footnote:

> Celsus knows, moreover, certain Marcellians, so called from Marcellina, and Harpocratians from Salome, and others who derive their name from Mariamne, and others again from Martha. We, however, who from a love of learning examine to the utmost of our ability not only the contents of Scripture, and the differences to which they give rise, but have also, from love to the truth, investigated as far as we could the opinions of philosophers, have never at any time met with these sects. [66]

The careful reader will note that the Greek does not read "Mariamne," but the very similar form, "Mariamme" (Μαριάμμης). But it is simply impossible to establish that Origen is, in fact, here making reference to Mary Magdalene! This is purely assumption and supposition on the part of scholars who are seeking only literary parallels, not facts of history. In fact, given the appearance immediately after of the name Martha, would it not be more logical to see this as a reference to the Mary referred to as the sister of Lazarus? In any case, Origen is thin ground upon which to make such a connection, as a brief reading of the text would prove. Might this be why Jacobovici and Tabor do not bother to give us the citation? One truly wonders.

Next we are referred to Epiphanius, but a scan of his works in the same scholarly resource (the *Thesaurus Linguae Graecae*) revealed no use of Mariamne/Mariamme at all. Instead, the connection drawn by some scholars is no stronger than that above with Origen. Reference is made to Epiphanius' work *Panarion*, also known as *Against Heresies*, written

---

[66] Origen, *Contra Celsus*, V:LXII, in Roberts and Donaldson, *The Ante-Nicene Fathers* (Grand Rapids: Eerdmans, 1982), IV:570. For the sake of completeness, the TLG reference follows with the form in question in bold:

> Contra Celsum 5.62.14 to   Contra Celsum 5.62.20 Κέλσος μὲν οὖν οἶδε καὶ Μαρκελλιανοὺς ἀπὸ Μαρκελλίνας καὶ Ἀρποκρατιανοὺς ἀπὸ Σαλώμης καὶ ἄλλους ἀπὸ **Μαριάμμης** καὶ ἄλλους ἀπὸ Μάρθας· ἡμεῖς δὲ οἱ διὰ τὴν κατὰ τὸ δυνατὸν ἡμῖν φιλομάθειαν οὐ μόνα τὰ ἐν τῷ λόγῳ καὶ τὰς διαφορὰς τῶν ἐν αὐτῷ ἐξετάσαντες, ἀλλ' ὅση δύναμις καὶ τὰ τῶν φιλοσοφησάντων φιλαλήθως ἐρευνήσαντες οὐδέ ποτε τούτοις ὡμιλήσαμεν.

around A.D. 375. Antti Marjanen, commenting on one of the key texts in Epiphanius relating to speculations about Mary Magdalene, writes:

> It is not altogether clear which Mary Epiphanius or the author of the *Questions of Mary* have in mind while writing the text. The fact that just a bit earlier Epiphanius had mentioned the mother of Jesus and called her the "ever-virgin Mary" (*Pan.* 26.7.5), while he later makes no effort to connect her with the episode he is describing suggests that Mary in this text is not Mary of Nazareth but the Magdalene.[67]

So even those who conclude Epiphanius is making reference to Mary Magdalene even in recounting the false views of heretics he is refuting have to admit that it is "not altogether clear" who he is referring to.[68] Thus far, then, we have a spelling in Origen that is different without any way of knowing if he is referring to Mary Magdalene, and speculations on who Epiphanius was referring to without ever using Mariamne at all! The threadbare nature of this argument is becoming all too evident.

Finally, we are referred to the Gnostic text, *Pistis Sophia,* from the late third to the early fourth century. No one will argue against the fact that the Gnostics made a great deal out of Mary Magdalene. But what is just as clear is that it is a gross historical error prompted by deep anti-Christian bias to ignore the historical disconnection between the Gnostic religion and the books produced by Gnostics in the second and third centuries. While it is all the rage to speculate about possible fragments of "tradition" to be found hidden in a phrase in the *Gospel of Thomas,* for example, the fact is that the Gnostics made things up out of whole cloth in seeking to establish a literary foundation for their religious beliefs while in conflict with orthodox Christianity. The onus is on the one citing these texts to demonstrate a reasonable basis for assuming anything they said has any relevance to first century Judea or

---

[67] Antti Marjanen, "The Mother of Jesus or the Magdalene? The Identity of Mary in the So-Called Gnostic Christian Texts" in *Which Mary? The Marys of Early Christian Tradition* (Leiden: Brill, 2002), p. 40.

[68] Marjanen includes a relevant footnote, "This does not mean that elements of the picture of Mary Magdalene remain unchangeable during the process of transmission. For example, in the *Manichaean Psalm-Book* Mary (Magdalene) is introduced as Martha's sister (192.23). The statement seems to derive from the period when at least the figures of Mary Magdalene and Mary of Bethany began to be fused together (41).

Galilee and the actual events of Jesus' life and ministry. Speculation doesn't cut it, but that is what we have in these sources. This is why we simply cannot give any credence to this kind of assertion, found in the words of Jacobovici:

> It is to noncanonical texts such as the Gnostic Gospel of Mary Magdalene and the Acts of Philip that we have to turn for a more complete profile. There she is a beloved apostle, a healer, a preacher, and a master in her own right. In the New Testament (1 Corinthians 16), Jesus too is referred to as "Mara" or "Master." In mirror fashion, in the Talpiot tomb the Mariamne inscription ends with the words: "also known as Mara."[69]

The Mary Magdalene of Gnosticism a hundred and fifty years later has precious little to do with the Mary Magdalene of Scripture, who happens to be the Mary Magdalene of history. The Gnostic Magdalene is a fictional character without roots in Judaism, without a real existence in Judea. The Gnostic Magdalene is an argument, a theology, not a human being who lived and witnessed the resurrection of Christ. Let Tabor and his fellows do the work of actually demonstrating that there is any reason at all to invest the slightest bit of historical weight into paper-thin connections they have attempted to forge between the Mary Magdalene of history and the Mariamne of a fourth-century work of fiction. They have not done this work, yet, they can provide the following kind of speculation with a straight face:

> Alternatively, isn't it also possible, as some scholars have suggested, that Mary Magdalene is often replaced in the Gospels by Mary, mother of Jesus, in order to obscure her role in Jesus's life? If this is the case, the incident at the cross can be reinterpreted as a dying man's last words to his wife ("woman"), not his mother, asking her to overcome her grief and protect their son from imminent danger.[70]

We have already had reason to note how outlandish this kind of speculation is. It not only has no historical foundation, but it likewise

---

[69] *TJFT*, 206.
[70] *TJFT*, 209.

presents the self-contradiction of exposing this alleged "family" to the Roman authorities they are supposedly so fearful of!

But let us lay this entire theory to rest by finally getting to the text and history of *The Acts of Philip* itself. Jacobovici and company give us next to no information about this work. They never quote from it outside of giving a reading from Francois Bovon that is not at all relevant to their theory. They do not explain how it is more relevant to the truth than John or Mark or Matthew or Luke or Paul. They simply assert it and expect to be believed.

First, *The Acts of Philip* is the work of the late fourth century Encratite community of Asia Minor. How do we know this? We know this because the book is clearly designed to defend a particular group and its beliefs, and we are able to identify, in history, the time period when this conflict took place, and where it was centered. Its time of origin, then, would be about A.D. 375 to A.D. 425. Its place of writing would be Asia Minor (not Jerusalem). And its author would be an Encratite monk or a community influenced by the Encratite movement.

The Encratites were a group that flourished during this period of time. They were identified by their rejection of "the flesh," meaning that they would not partake of meat (most held to some form of vegetarianism), wine, and procreation. Obviously, groups that deny the propriety of sexual intercourse and the production of children have a hard time staying in existence. But the Encratites, though they existed prior to the end of Roman persecution against Christians,[71] grew in numbers after the time of Constantine, possibly because of the formalism of the orthodox church, and the influx of those into the Christian church who had little concern about holiness or repentance of life.

As the Encratite movement gained in popularity, its teachings became subject to the scrutiny of the orthodox Christian church. In a provincial council called at Gangra in A.D. 340, the beliefs of Eustathius of Sebaste and his followers were addressed and condemned. There are numerous parallels between Eustathius' views and those expressed in

---

[71] Irenaeus in *Adv. Haer. 1:28:1* makes mention of the Encratites at the end of the second century in these words: "Springing from Saturninus and Marcion, those who are called Encratites (self-controlled) preached against marriage, thus setting aside the original creation of God, and indirectly blaming Him who made the male and female for the propagation of the human race. Some of those reckoned among them have also introduced abstinence from animal food, thus proving themselves ungrateful to God, who formed all things."

The Acts of Philip. Over the next forty or so years, the majority church took stronger action against the Encratites, and three Imperial decrees starting in A.D. 380 imposed restrictions on them. As their group began to feel more and more persecuted and marginalized, they developed their own means of defending themselves as well as encouraging their own followers in the face of hardship. *The Acts of Philip* grew out of the need for the Encratites to defend their views.

Some light is also shed on how late *The Acts of Philip* is in comparison to the canonical gospels (and hence how relevant it can possibly be to any kind of historical inquiry) by determining the first reference to the work in external documented sources. That is, when do we find anyone else citing or making reference to *The Acts of Philip?* Remember that the film dramatically presents hooded monks burning copies of the book in the second century, nearly two hundred years before it was even written! Time precluded an exhaustive search, but I was able to scan the *TLG* and *PL* databases and came to the conclusion that the earliest reference to *The Acts of Philip* is found in *The Decretum Gelasianum,* the catalog of accepted, and rejected, books traditionally attributed to Gelasius I, bishop of Rome from A.D. 492-496. There *The Acts of Philip* is listed alongside the acts of Andrew, Thomas, Peter, Matthias, Barnabas, etc.[72] By the midway point of the first millennium A.D. a whole series of such fictional works were circulating, all designed to promote the idiosyncratic viewpoints of small groups that had a bone to pick with the mainstream church, and, more so, with the Scriptures written by the closest followers of Jesus. I inquired of Francois Bovon,[73] and he likewise felt the reference in Gelasius is the earliest extant reference to *The Acts of Philip.*

It is fully understandable why Jacobovici and the others did not start out their argument, "Well, if you start with ascetic vegetarians in Asia Minor three hundred years after the time of Christ, you might discover something about how to identify inscriptions on ossuaries in Jerusalem, and therefore discover Jesus' family tomb!" And likewise, they were quite wise to avoid actually *quoting* the work. Why? There are two main reasons. First, *nowhere in the text do you find Mary Magdalene,* not once. Mariamne, yes, never Mary Magdalene. Secondly, the text is so ahistorical, so without value on that level, that to quote it would be self-destructive to the film and movie. For example, here is a portion of the text:

---

[72] *Patrologia Latina [CD-ROM] (Alexandria, VA: Chadwyk-Healey, 1995), 59:175.*
[73] E-mail of March 14, 2007.

125 They stripped and searched the apostles for charms, and pierced Philip's ankles and thighs and hung him head downward, and Bartholomew they hung naked by the hair. 126 And they smiled on each other, as not being tormented. But Mariamne on being stripped became like an ark of glass full of light and fire and every one ran away. 127 And Philip and Bartholomew talked in Hebrew, and Philip said: Shall we call down fire from heaven? 128 And now John arrived, and asked what was happening, and the people told him. 129 And he was taken to the place. Philip said to Bartholomew in Hebrew: Here is John the son of Barega (or, he that is in Barek), that is (or, where is) the living water. And John said: The mystery of him that hanged between the heaven and the earth be with you.

130 Then John addressed the people, warning them against the serpent. Inter alia: When all matter was wrought and spread out throughout the system of heaven, the works of God entreated God that they might see his glory: and when they saw it, their desire became gall and bitterness, and the earth became the storehouse of that which went astray, and the result and the superfluity of the creation was gathered together and became like an egg: and the serpent was born.[74]

The Mariamne of the Encratite imagination birthed three centuries after Christ could never, ever have been the wife of Jesus, for that was the very opposite of the whole purpose of her literary production! Instead, as Philip's sister, she is a powerful apostle and preacher. So powerful in fact, that, when threatened, she can turn into a glass box and frighten people away, as in these verses! She likewise…fights dragons. No one can seriously suggest that this text is actually relating historical traditions about Mary Magdalene. This is fiction, religious fiction, but fiction nonetheless. And it was written to encourage people to remain firm in their commitment to an ascetic lifestyle *that was directly opposed to the teachings of Christ and His apostles.*

Now, does it have to be emphasized that you do not determine the identities of those buried in multi-generational first century tombs in

---

[74] This is from the 1924 translation and is not based upon the Greek text Bovon found in 1974. But this will be the version more readily available to most. Francois Bovon has indicated to me that the English translation of his version of *The Acts of Philip* will be released in 2008.

Jerusalem on the basis of fourth century works of Encratite religious fiction from Asia Minor? And yet this is the very heart of the Jacobovici/Cameron film and book.

But, do they not provide the testimony of Francois Bovon? Yes, they do. And so I wrote to the good doctor. Here is our correspondence:

> March 7, 2007
> Dear Dr. Bovon:
>
> I am writing a response to the Jacobovici/Pellegrino work, and wished to ask for some brief words of clarification.
>
> On page 69 of Jacobovici/Pellegrino we read,
>
>> He handed me a folder containing copies of an ancient manuscript, penned in Greek, along with Professor Bovon's translation. The first page was headed by the words "Acts of Philip." In this text, Mary Magdalene was an apostle who preached and baptized and performed healing miracles. This Mary was very, very different from the Magdalene of Church doctrine, and not a "fallen woman" at all.
>> "Did you notice the Greek version of her name?" Simcha asked.
>> "According to the apostle Philip, who identifies himself as Mary's brother, she is not known as Magdalene, the 'woman from Magdala.' Rather, she is known by her given name, by the same word inscribed on the side of IAA 80/500: Mariamne."
>
> Then on page 96,
>
>> In June 2000, Bovon and Bouvier published the first complete translation—into French—of the Mount Athos version of the Acts of Philip, with its identification of Mary Magdalene as "Mariamne," the sister of the apostle Philip. The Acts of Philip provides us with a much more complete version of Mary Magdalene than the Gospels.

The book makes the statement that the Acts of Philip specifically, clearly, identifies Mariamne as Mary Magdalene. May I inquire:

1) Does the term Magdalene/Magdala appear anywhere in the Greek of the Acts of Philip?

2) Does the text of the Acts of Philip make the specific identification of Mariamne as Mary Magdalene?

3) If the answer to 2 is no, is it your position that this identification is founded upon certain parallels to Thomas and other gnostic literature, along with the Origen citation (*Contra Celsum* 5.62) using Mariamme?

Finally, sir, do you feel your position, and your words, has been accurately represented in both the documentary and the published book?

Thank you for your attention.

March 8, 2007
Dear Dr. White,

I thank you for your message. I am pleased to answer your questions. First, the name Magdala does not appear in the Acts of Philip. Second, no, since the woman apostle is called during the whole text Mariamne. Mariamne is a possible Greek for the Semitic name Myriam. And the woman acts in the apocryphal book as Mary Magdalene in non canonical stories. Third, I believe yes, but I place myself on the level of literary traditions and not on the level of history. I believe that the Acts of Philip carry old traditions concerning a strong woman disciple of Jesus.

Here is what I sent to another colleague, it may interest you:

"In these interviews I said that I was not convinced by the program. I thought that the filmmaker has two speeches: on the one hand he expresses his wish to open a scholarly discussion; on the other he realizes his personal agenda. I said also that the final part with Jesus' marriage and having a child is just science fiction. I added that the film should deal with the very old tradition of the holy sepulcher which remains for me the best location for Jesus' tomb since the emperor Constantine built this monument at the spot where the emperor Hadrian erected a statue to himself and another for Jupiter in the second century to humiliate the Christians who venerated Jesus' tomb at this place. I said finally concerning Mariamne that this name is a possible equivalent to the Semitic name Myriam, besides Maria and Mariam (I did not say that this was the real name of Mary of Magdala), and that the traditions concerning Mariamne in the Acts of Philip coincides with what we learn from this women in the New Testament and non canonical texts. I said that the Acts of Philip sends her to the Jordan Valley, but the filmmaker concludes that this means Jerusalem! I have published sufficiently in New Testament Studies in 1984, in the book Which Mary? ed. F. Stanley Jones and in the Festschrift for Elisabeth Schüssler Fiorenza as well as in Aufstieg und Niedergang der römischen Welt in 1988 plus the critical edition of the Acts of Philip in the Series apocryphorum of the Corpus Christianorum (Turnhout: Brepols, 1999) in order my position to be known by scholars."

Sincerely,
François Bovon

Please note some of the key statements from Dr. Bovon:

- The name Magdala does not appear in the text of *The Acts of Philip*.
- The text of *The Acts of Philip* does not identify Mariamne with Mary Magdalene.
- Bovon's identification of Mariamne with Mary Magdalene is relevant only on the level of *literary tradition* and not on the level of *history*.
- The idea of Jesus and Mary Magdalene having a child is "science fiction."
- He did not say the real name of Mary Magdalene is Mariamne.
- The Jordan Valley is not Jerusalem!

Bovon believes there are literary traditions, familiar to the writer of *The Acts of Philip*, where the author encountered a strong woman disciple of Jesus. In the Gnostic writings, this would be Mary Magdalene, herself, as noted above, a fictionalized character that was likewise dependent upon an earlier source, that being the canonical Gospels. The writer, then, familiar with these previous literary traditions, weaves them together into a new person, Mariamne, who then acts in such a way as to encourage and defend Encratite values. She becomes, then, an apologetic argument for the minority Encratite community of the late fourth century in Asia Minor. But this is a literary tradition, *not a historical person*. It is simply absurd on its face to say:

> Because of the Gnostic gospels, because of the Acts of Phillip - several ancient texts that have recently been discovered, the *Acts of Philip* in the seventies. Scholars agree what Mary Magdalene's real name is, and her name is Mariamne.[75]

Obviously, scholars recognize that you do not use fictional characters from fourth-century texts in Asia Minor to identify inscriptions on ossuaries found in first-century tombs in Jerusalem. But that is what Jacobovici and Pellegrino and Tabor and Cameron have asked us to believe. And sadly, many will believe them, too.

Now you have the information you need to recognize the very heart of this theory for what it truly is: a well-funded, nicely produced *myth*. Since this part of the argument fails, the rest falls. And while the argument truly is over at this point, we will surely press forward in our inquiry so as to document the lengths to which men will go to find a way to fill the empty tomb of Jesus.

---

[75] Simcha Jacobovici, *Discovery Channel Interview*.

DNA: The Fingerprint of God

CSI: Crime Scene Investigators has become a cultural phenomenon in the United States and around the world. Though not exactly realistic in everything seen on the program, still it manages to provide an amazing amount of education while entertaining the audience. Sometimes I wonder if people have not learned more about science from Gill Grissom than they did while in school. If so, kudos to Grissom.

You cannot watch an episode of *CSI* without hearing about DNA, which is, of course, deoxyribonucleic acid, the very blueprint of life itself. When in college, I double-majored in Bible and Biology (minor in Greek). My senior year, I was department fellow in Anatomy and Physiology, and my senior project was in genetics. I found in the DNA transcription mechanisms of living organisms, one of the most convicting evidences of God's existence right there in each cell of my body. Studying that interactively complex mechanism convinced me that anyone who tries to explain living beings without reference to a wise and powerful God is truly no more insightful than the pot which loudly proclaims "there is no Potter!"

When the tomb story broke, I was immediately faced with the claims being made regarding DNA analysis of the ossuaries from the Talpiot tomb. My thoughts turned to the reality we face in Western societies today. Most have been taught that science is unquestionable, unbiased, and "true" by definition. Religion must be questionable at every point, all religious people are biased and unreliable, and religion is mere "opinion." In light of this reality, the claim that DNA evidence "proves" important elements of the Jacobovici theory would be heard as carrying a tremendous amount of weight. Aside from O.J., hasn't DNA pretty much reigned supreme? So if DNA proves this is Jesus' family tomb, Christianity needs to simply fold up its tent and put an "Out of Business" sign on the front door.

But just what is the truth regarding the DNA "evidence" presented by Jacobovici and his fellows? It did not take long to find out. Once again, we need to see how far our theorists have been willing to go in their promotion of their theory. At the press conference announcing the "discovery," replayed later on the program hosted by Ted Koppel after the initial airing of the film, Simcha Jacobovici addressed the DNA evidence taken from "human debris" found in the bottom of Talpiot ossuaries 80-500 and 80-503 (those identified by the inscriptions Yeshua bar Yosef and Mariame kai Mara, theorized in the film to be Mary Magdalene). He said, "The forensic archaeologist concluded that they must be husband and wife." Is it true that Dr. Carney Matheson concluded that the inhabitants of those ossuaries "must be husband and wife"? Can DNA evidence derived from ancient ossuaries provide that kind of information? Despite the widespread knowledge of the *existence* of DNA, very few know almost anything about it on a scientific level, so these kinds of claims carry tremendous weight, *but only out of ignorance.*

Off to Thunder Bay

I am told you have to be a real Canadian to live in Thunder Bay, Ontario. I live in Phoenix, Arizona, just about the polar opposite, temperature-wise. In any case, Lakehead University is located there, and boasts one of the top DNA laboratories in the world. In particular, they are experts in extracting, amplifying, and sequencing DNA from ancient sources, which is, of course, very demanding work. Dr. Carney Matheson heads up the lab there at Lakehead University.

Jacobovici and Pellegrino came up with the idea of seeing if the small amounts of "human debris" in two of the ossuaries could yield enough DNA for sampling. One of the major myths circulating about this story is that the bones of Jesus have been found. It should be remembered that the bones from all the ossuaries were buried back in 1980. All that would remain would be chips, splinters, tiny fragments locked in the debris clinging to the sides and bottom of the ossuaries. 2000 year old gunk, to put it kindly.

Much has been made of the fact that only two ossuaries were tested, 80-500 ("Mariamne") and 80-503 (Yeshua). The producers claim that, for example, the Judah ossuary had been in essence "vacuumed out," leaving no debris to test. But in other instances, a lack of funds was cited. In any case, we might well hear of future studies done on these ossuaries, for clearly certain results could completely disprove the theory thus far propounded.

When the samples were submitted to Matheson's lab, they were simply marked 80-500 and 80-503. As expected, they were not able to extract nuclear DNA from the samples. Nuclear DNA is the substance found in the nucleus that is normally associated with what you hear about obtaining a "DNA match" in criminal investigations. Nuclear DNA degrades very quickly and is especially susceptible to contamination. Two thousand years of changing weather, insects, and the like almost guarantees nuclear DNA will be destroyed.

But there is another source of DNA.[76] The "power house" of the cell is called the mitochondrion. This amazing structure is the primary location of the biochemical reactions that provide the power (in the form of adenosine triphosphate, or ATP) for all cellular activities. The mitochondria are very hardy little structures, and each cell contains many of them. Though the DNA found in the mitochondria is much "simpler" than that found in the nucleus (and hence carries less information), since there is so much more of it due to the many mitochondria in the cell, it is easier to find traces of it after a very long period of time. Most of the ancient DNA extracted today is mitochondrial DNA. However, mitochondrial DNA also differs from nuclear DNA in that it is passed down only through the maternal line, from the mother. But, what you *can* do with mitochondrial DNA is rule out certain kinds of relationships between samples. And that is what Dr. Matheson did up in cold, cold Thunder Bay.

---

[76] John M. Butler, *Forensic DNA Typing* (2nd Ed.: Biology, Technology, and Genetics of STR Markers (Academic Press, 2005), 241, 249:

> The primary characteristic that permits its recovery from degraded samples is the fact that mtDNA is present in cells at a much higher copy number than the nuclear DNA from which STRs are amplified. In short, though nuclear DNA contains much more information, there are only two copies of it in each cell (one maternal and one paternal) while mtDNA has a bit of useful genetic information times hundreds of copies per cell. With a higher copy number, some mtDNA molecules are more likely to survive than nuclear DNA….The circular nature of mtDNA makes it less susceptible to exonucleases that break down DNA molecules needed to survive until forensic DNA testing can be completed. The presence of an increased number of mtDNA molecules per cell relative to the nuclear DNA chromosomes also enhances the mtDNA survival rate, as does the fact that they are encapsulated in a two-walled organelle.

Here is the story as it is related in the book. After informing Jacobovici and Pellegrino that they could not extract nuclear DNA, we pick up the story:

> "However," Matheson said, "we did not quit. Instead, we shifted our focus to the mitochondrial DNA—which is, of course, the DNA inherited maternally, from mother to child. This means that we can identify maternal relationships. Meaning, we can only address questions such as: 'Are these two individuals—one male and the other female—mother and child? Are they brother and sister? Or are they two unrelated individuals?'" Carney fell silent.[77]

Please note what Dr. Matheson says.   Maternal relationships. Mother/child.   Brother/sister (same mother).   But *only* maternal relationships.   Paternal relationships (father/daughter, for example), *cannot be detected by analysis of mitochondrial DNA.*

> "So," Matheson continued, "when we see a number of polymorphisms between two sequences, we can then conclude that these two individuals are not related—or, at least, not maternally related." Simcha and Tabor were now both smiling broadly, though Dr. Matheson did not yet know why. "And," said Simcha, "this means—?"

> "That this man and woman do not share the same mother," Matheson said quickly and conclusively. "They cannot be mother and child. They cannot, maternally, be brother and sister. And so, for these particular samples, because they come from the same tomb—and we suspect it to be a familial tomb— these two individuals, if they were unrelated, would most likely have been husband and wife."[78]

As we will see below, Dr. Matheson regrets that last line, but even then, it is clear he is speculating, not *concluding* anything based upon the evidence. For you see, there is a relationship that could exist between the ossuaries tested that for some odd reason is never explicitly noted by Jacobovici and Pellegrino: father and daughter. I believe it would be

---

[77] *TJFT*, 170.
[78] *TJFT*, 172.

incumbent upon the authors to clearly, forcefully explain this possibility, but they do not. There are others, too. This was a multi-generational tomb. Thirty-five people are estimated to be present. Clearly, you could have cousins and nephews and servants and the like, not just a relationship of father and daughter. The functioning presupposition seems to be that we have here a "nuclear" family, but that simply does not fit with the other tombs excavated in Jerusalem. I do not believe Matheson was apprised, from the start, of the possibility of not only multiple people in the ossuaries, but of thirty-five people in the tomb as a whole.

Even so, Matheson made sure to emphasize *maternal* relationships. So why did Jacobovici and his team ignore this restriction? Because they had already come to their conclusions. They had bought the Mary Magdalene/Mariamne story hook, line, and sinker, and now they were on their way to proving it. Note, for example:

> Impossible. But the details extracted from the tomb so far had failed consistently to negate the conclusion and were in fact adding up, one positive indicator after another, in support of it. They had begun to read the DNA of Jesus and Mary Magdalene. Unimaginable. But there it was.[79]

Note the reasoning expressed in the odd expression, "failed consistently to negate the conclusion." The conclusion already existed, and each test was just a means of dodging the bullet that would kill the conclusion. *This is not how scholarship is done.* Yes, they had begun to read the [mitochondrial] DNA of a Yeshua [sixth most popular name at the time for men] from Jerusalem [if the ossuary only had one person in it] and Mariame [or Martha or someone else whose bones might have been in the same ossuary] which only showed that the donors of the [mitochondrial] DNA were not maternally related. That is not *nearly* as exciting as the way it is put in the book, is it? But, it is far more truthful. It is the "drama" of the story that is used to cover over the gaping holes in the logic and scholarship of this theory. Pellegrino writes at one point:

> About 7:00 p.m., I arrived in New York City and was heading home for supper, timed to the latest episode of a TV program called *24*. On my way to a bus stop, I passed a

---

[79] *TJFT*, 173.

familiar street preacher who ministered to the homeless and who had always called out to me the same greeting: "Have you found Jesus, brother?"

I nodded to him and gave the usual reply: "I'm working on it."

Several times before, I had strolled under the lights near Broadway and Times Square with samples from the Talpiot tomb in my carrying case. This night, for the first time, it occurred to me that no one walking by me on the sidewalks of Manhattan would have believed that the most secret (and perhaps most sacred) artifacts in the world were passing within just a few paces of them. The most deeply hidden secret of military think-tankers was more widely known than the fact that DNA and apparent remnants of Jesus's shroud had come to New York.[80]

There is no question that these men seem to have fully bought into their own theory. They really do believe their conclusions. They believe they have in fact disproved the heart of the Christian faith. But in reality, they have only proven that there is no limitation to how far people will go to spin the facts to fit their desired conclusions.

Later in the book Jacobovici wraps up the story and writes as part of his summary:

> Dr. Matheson and his team were not able to extract nuclear DNA from the degraded samples. However, they were able to extract mitochondrial DNA from both the Jesus and Mariamne ossuaries. This allowed them to confirm that these were indeed Middle Eastern people of antiquity and that they were *not* related.[81]

Not *maternally* related is such a restrictive viewpoint, why bother with it? Let's just expand that out to simply "not related" because that fits our theory that Mariamne is Mary Magdalene, and without this piece of information, how can we shoot those touching scenes with Jesus and Mary Magdalene and little Judah? Starting with your conclusions can be very comfortable, but it is also the single best way to make sure that the arguments you use to get there will be completely invalid, as in this case.

---

[80] *TJFT*, 191.
[81] *TJFT*, 207.

Dr. Matheson Clarifies

Shortly after the story broke, I inquired of a friend who is a CSI who works with DNA about the nature of the kinds of tests that could be run on "debris" 2,000 years old. She confirmed that it was most likely a mitochondrial DNA extraction, and then she managed to get in contact with Dr. Carney Matheson directly, who confirmed her thoughts. I then took the opportunity to contact Dr. Matheson. I would like to note that Dr. Matheson was always quite prompt in responding to my inquiries, and that despite this statement about him in the book:

> Days turned to weeks, and weeks to months, before Matheson, who doesn't own a cell phone and rarely checks e-mails, called Tabor back. They had successfully extracted DNA. Simcha and Tabor gave him an unprecedented response: "Don't tell us the results over the phone. We're coming up as fast as we can. We're coming with a camera crew. Tell us then."[82]

In any case, I wrote to Dr. Matheson on March 2, 2007:

> Dear Dr. Matheson:
>
> I am sure you are deluged at the moment on the tomb issue, so I will be very brief. I appreciate any response you can offer.
>
> On page 172 of *The Jesus Family Tomb* you are quoted as follows:
>
> > "That this man and woman do not share the same mother," Matheson said quickly and conclusively. "They cannot be mother and child. They cannot, maternally, be brother and sister. And so, for these particular samples, because they come from the same tomb—and we suspect it to be a familial tomb—these two individuals, if they were unrelated, would most likely have been husband and wife."
>
> Given that mitochondrial DNA analysis can only address maternal relationships, leaving open the possibility that 80-503 was, in fact, the father of 80-500, and the mitochondrial DNA analysis could not address this, is the preceding quotation

---

[82] *TJFT*, 168.

accurate to your recollection? Did you inform Simcha Jacobovici of the possible paternal relationship?

He replied *the same day*:

> March 2, 2007
>
> Dear James White,
>
> This work was done as a service. We did not know who they suspected these individuals to be from. On the report it concludes that these two profiles from two different individuals were not maternally related. That is all the report states. When they did the filming and on the documentary they asked every question under the sun with permutations and manipulations. I provided the investigators with all the possibilities. They were not brother and sister, mother and child, maternal cousins, maternal grandparent and child etc. I also mentioned all of the possibilities, which I should not have done in hindsight. These included, father and daughter, paternal cousins, half brother and sister (sharing the same father) or simply unrelated individuals.
>
> The media does what they want.

According to Dr. Matheson, he did inform them of the possibility of the other relationships, including "father and daughter, paternal cousins, half brother and sister," etc. Were the cameras rolling then? Didn't get a good enough angle or have proper lighting to include that in the film? Or did it just not make the "cut" for the film? In any case, Matheson has confirmed that the other possibilities, which mysteriously vanish from the book and film, were provided to Jacobovici and Pellegrino. Those buying into this conspiracy should be made fully aware of the realities of the DNA testing.

A week later I had another thought that I felt was worth running by Dr. Matheson. I was collating the information about the number of people buried in the tomb and wondered about the impact this might have upon the testing. So I wrote again:

> March 10, 2007
> Dear Dr. Matheson:
>
> A very, very brief follow up, please. I know you must be very tired of this, but I have not read any clarification of what would seem to me to be a very central point.

The initial archaeological reports on the Talpiot tomb estimated 1.7 bodies/ossuary (Kloner 1996). All I have read so far has seemed to assume a single skeleton in each ossuary, 80-500 and 80-503. Were you informed prior to your testing of the possibility of multiple sources of DNA in the ossuaries, i.e., multiple individuals in a single ossuary? If there were, in fact, two or more individuals represented in the human remains found in 80-500 and in 80-503, would this have impacted the methodology you used? Would it impact the amplification process? If you were not informed, would it now impact the results provided to Jacobovici and Pellegrino?

Once again, I deeply thank you for your patience in this matter. This question seems central and obvious, but I have not seen any discussion of it at all.

I sent this late in the evening, and by the next day Dr. Matheson had kindly responded once again:

March 11, 2007

Dear James White,

It is interesting that there might have been more than one body per ossuary. This is actually pretty common in other ossuaries. However the methodology that we employed would be able to identify this possibility. Unlike forensic DNA typing where you do a profile and that is all. We used Forensic protocols and ancient DNA criteria. Ancient DNA criteria requires that you clone the PCR product and by doing this we would be able to identify a mixture of two or more individuals. This was done in this case.

As you can see there are many scientific aspects not explained by these researchers which would be nice to have answers.

Yes, Dr. Matheson is correct. Many unanswered questions, but most of them center on why these researchers chose to 1) spin the facts they had, 2) ignore other facts that did not fit their conclusions, and 3) rush to judgment. Had they vetted their claims in the proper scholarly domains, these issues would have immediately come to light and, at the very least, the claims modified and reduced to fit the data on hand. But all one has to do is look at the "Lost Tomb of Jesus" website[83] and you will see why they did not take this approach. It would not sell.

Let's summarize. The donor of the "human debris" in ossuary 80-500 found in the Talpiot tomb (possibly one of multiple persons in the ossuary, probably the first one placed therein) was not maternally related to the donor of the "human debris" in ossuary 80-503. There is your "DNA" evidence. Nothing more. These tests cannot rule out a father/daughter relationship, for example, or any other non-maternal relationship, let alone extended non-maternal family, especially loved servants, etc. The application made by the book (the insinuation of a married relationship between Jesus of Nazareth and Mary Magdalene), dependent as it is upon identifying Mariamne as Mary Magdalene, has already been debunked, rendering the "see, they could be married!" argument irrelevant. And so all the talk of DNA comes down to just this: two folks in a tomb were not maternally related. And that is not news.

---

[83] http://www.jesusfamilytomb.com/

Statistics and the Jerusalem Phone Book

Did you know that 87.9% of all statistics are misused? It's true! Well, it's true 78.4% of the time anyway, right?

We are deluged with statistics every day. I have even read that it is far more likely that someone will believe you if you use a decimal in your percentages more often than if you round it out. So, if you say "74% of people believe this," you will get less traction than if you say "73.8% of people believe this." Our relationship to odds, statistics, percentages, and the like is an uneasy one.

Most of us are not mathematicians. Most of us picked on those who were back in grade school on the playground. Now they are getting us back. Every time you tune into a news show today, you feel like you are at the mercy of mathematicians. Often we suspect something is not quite right, but who really knows?

After creating a ridiculously flimsy connection through literary parallels to a group of vegetarian ascetics in the fourth century and then back in time to a first-century ossuary with multiple possible readings of its inscription, spinning DNA evidence and creating a conclusion never offered by the actual science, our intrepid group of theorists finishes off its argument by a bogus appeal to the science of statistics and probability. Do not get me wrong: the math is correct. That isn't the problem. The problem is that probabilities have to start somewhere. They need a set of starting data. And given that the mathematicians were given the data set we have already examined, replete with their flawed conclusions, the result was completely predictable. They had a 100% chance of completely missing the point.

Let's look at the argument and then examine the starting point that illustrates yet again that mathematical probabilities are only as good as the starting assumptions upon which they are calculated:

> It would all come down to statistics, I figured. After the story came out, after the requisite howls of derision, rewriting of history and retraction of statements, the facts of the Talpiot tomb would stand. They were simply too clear cut. And then, it would come down to statistics. "What are the odds," people would ask, "that the Talpiot tomb really belongs to Jesus of Nazareth, and not some other Jesus?"[84]

Indeed, what are the odds? And how do you determine the "odds" of finding tombs build 2,000 years ago? What is the process? Pellegrino laid out the odds in *The Jesus Family Tomb* as follows. First, you start with a source of names:

> According to scholars such as L. Y. Rahmani, Tal Ilan, and Rachael Hachlili, Jesus and Joseph were common names in first-century Jerusalem; for example, among the 233 inscribed ossuaries cataloged by the IAA, the name Joseph appeared 14 percent of the time and Jesus appeared 9 percent. It is estimated that, at most, during the entire period of ossuary use in Jerusalem the male population was 80,000. Out of these, 7,200 would have been called Jesus and 11,200 would have been called Joseph. Multiplying the percentages against each other (.09 × .14 × 80,000), we get 1,008 men who would have been called Jesus, son of Joseph during the century of ossuary use. In other words, approximately one in 79 males was called Jesus, son of Joseph. On my white pad, I wrote: "1 out of 79."[85]

I note in passing that limiting your basis only to ossuaries seems a bit arbitrary. Why not use other literary sources as well, such as Josephus? And please note, this is limited solely to Jerusalem. I will repeatedly note a fact that truly seems to have missed Jacobovici, Pellegrino, Cameron, Tabor, etc. The name is Jesus of Nazareth, not Jesus of *Jerusalem*. In case your geography is a bit hazy, it is 120 miles from Jerusalem to Nazareth. While that is not overly far in modern terms, try walking it. It is a major trip. So, from the start, a simple observation:

---

[84] *TJFT*, 74.
[85] Ibid.

we are starting with the assumption that there *was* a Jesus family tomb in Jerusalem, and, it has been discovered (remember, many tombs exist like the one noted, but not entered, by Jacobovici only 20 meters from the Talpiot tomb). Pellegrino continues:

> But how many of those 1,008 men living right before, during, and after the time of Jesus of Nazareth were buried with a Maria or a Judah or a Matthew?
>
> From this point onward, the "Jesus equation" was simply a matter of factoring the probability of each name in the tomb cluster, one after the other, and multiplying them against each other.
>
> Professor Tal Ilan records 8 Marias on 193 ossuaries. Therefore, approximately one out of 24 females was called Maria. So I wrote "1 out of 24" on my white pad.[86]

You can see the outline of the process now. Look at the current listing of ossuaries, determine your percentages from that, and multiply the factors together to determine your odds. But our theorists were aware of the fact that there are many variables to be considered in such a calculation:

> Professor Camille Fuchs, a professor of statistics at Tel Aviv University, said that in evaluating ossuary inscriptions of this kind, we have to remember that only a small elite could afford family crypts and that inscribed ossuaries represented literate people, who themselves were a fraction of the Jerusalem population at the time. Had I lowered the population of Jerusalem during the period of ossuary use by limiting our investigation to well-to-do literate people, the numbers would have played too strongly in our favor. I decided to ignore both wealth and literacy.

I note this discussion for two reasons: "only a small elite could afford family crypts." Though the film and book make it appear that Jesus would have had the monetary standing to allow for the construction of a multi-generational family tomb, no evidence is presented to substantiate such a viewpoint. In point of fact, the Gospels tell us just the opposite. They tell us he did not even own his own home, was itinerant, and when visiting Jerusalem, slept with his disciples on the Mount of Olives,

---

[86] Ibid., 75.

probably in a cave that has been found that was used for producing olive oil. There is simply no evidence offered for assuming that Jesus was amongst the elite of Jerusalem; there is no evidence offered for assuming he would build a multi-generational tomb in Jerusalem under the noses of his most inveterate enemies rather than in Nazareth, or even *somewhere* in Galilee, like Capernaum. And note again the limitation of these compilations to residents of Jerusalem. *Jesus was not a resident of Jerusalem.* He did not live there. He was a resident of a town one hundred and twenty miles away, a good week's journey by foot. One might ask why the calculation continued, given this basic historical fact which, it would seem *precludes* Jesus as a possibility!

> At this point in my statistical analysis, my probability factor held at one in 2.5 million. Meaning, the odds were 2.5 million to one in favor of the Talpiot tomb being the tomb of Jesus of Nazareth.[87]

2,500,000 : 1! That's a huge number. That *must* mean this is the Jesus family tomb, right? Well, not quite. It sounds good, but, as the close reader has already seen, the foundation of the calculations is open to a wide variety of questions that would materially impact the conclusions. The book did not stick with Pellegrino's calculation but took the same information (and the same foundational assumptions) to Dr. Andrey Feuerverger of the University of Toronto. He did his calculations based upon the assertions we have already examined regarding Mariamne/Mary Magdalene, for example:

> Feuerverger was especially impressed (on a mathematical level) with the "Mariamne-Mara" inscription. "That," he said, "is an extremely unusual one—with a Magdalene connection from the Acts of Philip, a connection that appears to convey that she belongs in this tomb."[88]

Feuerverger's numbers were smaller simply because he reduced the factors in light of recognizing that not all tombs have been discovered, for example. But what he did not do is analyze the starting assumption, specifically that there *is* a Jesus family tomb to be found in Jerusalem in the first place. It likewise accepts the Mariamne connection, which we have seen is utterly without merit and historically unfounded.

---

[87] *TJFT*, 82.
[88] *TJFT*, 112.

Feuerverger, as a mathematician, would not be expected to examine the historical propriety of *The Acts of Philip* connection. We cannot know what his calculations would be were he to have the full picture. His "low end" number, *based upon the Mariamne/Mary Magdalene* connection, is 600:1 in favor of the tomb being that of Jesus. It is important to note his own words on this subject, as provided in an e-mail sent to Ted Koppel:

> I must work from the interpretations given to me, and the strength of the calculations are based on those assumptions…If for some reason one were to read it as just a regular form of Maria, in that case the calculation produced is not as impressive, and the statistical significance would wash out considerably.

Given the readings of the inscription already provided, here the film's own expert undercuts the key element of this statistical argument. Yet, you will continue to hear the 600:1 number for a long time to come.

Regarding the foundational issue, whether there would be a Jesus family tomb to be found, note this:

> And yet—and this may come as a surprise to most readers— scholars are happy to connect ossuaries with leading characters from the Gospels as long as they are not related to Jesus or his family. For example, ten years after the Talpiot tomb was found, a bulldozer revealed the name Caiaphas in a tomb near Jerusalem's Peace Forest. An announcement then went out— from the scholarly community—that the family tomb of the Temple high priest who persecuted Jesus had been found. The story made headline news internationally.[89]

Do our theorists have a point here? Are archaeologists operating on the double standard that they allege exists? Is there something wrong with accepting the Caiaphas ossuary while rejecting the Jesus identification? Surely not. There is every reason to believe Caiaphas would have a tomb in Jerusalem. *He wasn't called Caiaphas of Nazareth.* That's the whole point! You would fully expect Caiaphas to be buried amongst the elites of Jerusalem *because he was one of Jerusalem's elite.* Jesus was not.

As soon as I heard Jacobovici presenting his argumentation, I knew there was something missing in what he was saying. Would it not be the case that if you looked at almost any tomb that has been found,

---

[89] *TJFT*, 117.

and if you were to start multiplying the probability factors of finding any particular name, that the resultant numbers would be high for *any* family? And if these calculations had been done a number of years ago when, for example, half as many ossuaries had been discovered, wouldn't this produce completely different numbers? It would seem so. But once the actual argumentation became public knowledge, other credentialed mathematicians had the opportunity of examining Feuerverger's conclusions.

David Stamps has a Ph.D. in Applied Mathematics from the University of Missouri – St. Louis, and he did his dissertation in the field of probability theory. He was kind enough to simplify the mathematical science and lay out the assumptions inherent in the argument based upon Feuerverger's calculations:

> There are 3 events which must occur for the tomb to be that of the family of Jesus:
>
> A: The family of Jesus had a tomb in the city of Jerusalem (or nearby)
>
> B: Given that A is true, the tomb has been discovered
>
> C: Given that both A and B are true, the tomb is the one belonging to the family of Jesus (as opposed to others in Jerusalem).
>
> The probability of an event, say the probability that A is true will be written: P(A)
>
> So, we want to compute: P(A and B and C are all true)
>
> P(A and B and C occur) = P(C given that both A and B are true) * P(B given that A is true) * P(A is true)
>
> In statistics, the word "given," denoting a conditional probability, is represented by the symbol: |
>
> So: P(A and B and C occur) = P(C | A and B are true) * P(B | A is true) * P(A is true)
>
> Dr. Feuerverger's estimate (599/600) is actually the product: P(C | A and B are true) * P(B | A is true)
>
> He has done this by assuming that the "already discovered" tombs are ¼ of the total.
>
> So: P(A and B and C occur) = (599/600) * P(A is true)

This last probability is entirely neglected in his analysis (and can drastically reduce the final result). This is even conceding the validity of the number 599/600, which is debatable.

So, if the probability that a family of the make-up of Jesus' family (and residing in Nazareth) has a family tomb in the near vicinity of Jerusalem, the final probability is drastically reduced.[90]

So the point that needs to be emphasized is this: what is the value of P(A is true)? What is the probability that a visitor to Jerusalem, hated by the religious leadership of the city, who predicted the destruction of the Temple located there, who had no sources of funding, who clearly lived elsewhere (Galilee, Nazareth, in particular, but who also had close ties to another city we can locate historically, Capernaum), would possess a multi-generational family tomb 120 miles away from his home? Personally, I would say there is no chance at all. So, factor that into the equation, along with the proper reading of the Mariame ossuary, and you are left with…absolutely nothing. Zero. "Statistical insignificance" would be the proper term.

More About the Jerusalem Phonebook

In pursuit of providing needed background information, while at the same time illustrating the "spin" Jacobovici and his team have put on their presentation, we note a few important facts regarding the names found in various sources regarding ancient Israel. Ironically, one of the sources is noted in the tomb book itself, that being the work of Bellarmino Bagatti. The tomb book employs Bagatti's work in excavating *Dominus Flevit* (an ancient graveyard in Jerusalem) to bolster its argumentation that there is a willingness upon the part of academia to hold to long established theories in the face of new data (such as their own). One of the stories told relates to the finding of an ossuary in *Dominus Flevit* with the inscription "Simon bar Jonah," the specific name of Jesus' disciple Peter.

While it is indeed very interesting to note the existence of this ossuary, what should trouble the fair-minded reader is the fact that Jacobovici and Pellegrino did not see fit to let their audience know a little something about the *other* names found on ossuaries in *Dominus Flevit*. They took cameras into the graveyard itself to attempt to substantiate the idea that the ornamental symbol over the Talpiot tomb

---

[90] Personal e-mail from Dr. Stamps to James White, March 8, 2007.

is somehow related to the Judeo-Christian community. So it is hard to believe they are not familiar with the actual contents. What are some of the other names found there? Would it not interest their audience to know that Mary, Martha, Joseph, Matthew, *and Jesus*, have all been found in the inscriptions on the ossuaries in *Dominus Flevit?* Surely they were aware of this, but it would hardly help their theory to report all the facts in this instance. In fact, here is a listing of names (in Italian) provided by Bagatti:[91]

Nome proprio		Egitto	Giuseppe	Ossuari	N. Test.	Murabba'àt
Simeone	(5)	ca 33	29	32	9	ca 14+7
Giuseppe	(20)	32	19	23	8	10+9
Salome	(8)	—	3	21	1	+3
Giuda	(13)	11	14	20	7	5+4
Maria	(7)	3	7	19	7	4+1
Giovanni	(18)	13	13	19	6	9+1
Eleazar	(25)	7	21	17	3	3+4
Gesù	(29)	12	15	13	4	6+6
Marta	(7)	2		9	1	—
Mattia	(3)		—	7	1	+1
Safira	(13)			7	1	—
Gionata	(16)	7	11	5	1	9+2
Zaccaria	(30)	3	2	4	1	
Azaria	(30)	1	1	4		—
Giairo	(1)	1	1	2	1	
Menahem	(22)	—	2	2	1	4+

The names listed here include Simon, Joseph, Salome, Judas, Maria, John, Eleazar, Jesus, Martha, Matthew, Sapphira, Jonathan, Zechariah and James. Why would our authors not inform their readers and viewers of the existence of ossuaries bearing these kinds of names right in Jerusalem itself? Could it be because this would dilute the attention they are intent upon creating on *their* tomb, the Talpiot tomb? One can only speculate.

Recall what we noted earlier:

---

[91] http://biblelight.net/DF-pg-108.gif

After all, because of the existence of ossuaries, we have a veritable phonebook of Jerusalem's political, economic, and religious elite dating back to the time of Jesus.[92]

What can we learn from this "phonebook"? Based on the information provided by Richard Bauckham,[93] here are the top ten names for men amongst Palestinian Jews, 330 B.C. to A.D. 200. The total valid names include references in literature such as the New Testament, Josephus, etc., combined with those found on ossuaries.

Name	Total Valid	On Ossuaries	% of Total
1. Simon/Simeon	243	59	9.3
2. Joseph/Joses	218	45	8.3
3. Lazarus/Eleazar	166	29	6.3
4. Judas/Judah	164	44	6.2
5. John/Yohanan	122	25	4.6
6. Jesus/Joshua	99	22	3.8
7. Ananias/Hananiah	82	18	3
8. Jonathan	71	14	2.7
9. Matthew/Matthias	62	17	2.4
10. Manaen	42	4	1.6

And here are the same numbers for the names of women in the same time period, same sources.

Name	Total Valid	On Ossuaries	% of Total
1. Mary/Mariam	70	42	21.7
2. Salome	58	41	17.7
3. Shelamzion	24	19	7.3
4. Martha	20	17	6.1
5. Sapphira	12	7	3.7
6. Berenice	8	1	2.4
7. Imma	7	6	2.1
8. Mara	7	5	2.1
9. Cyprus	6	0	1.8
10. Sarah	6	3	1.8

---

[92] *TJFT*, 28.
[93] Richard Bauckham, *Jesus and the Eyewitnesses: The Gospels as Eyewitness Testimony* (Grand Rapids: Eerdmans, 2006), pp. 85-91. Bauckham is utilizing, but likewise filtering, the data from Ilan's *Lexicon*.

We immediately note a glaring factor: we have 1269 references to men constituting the "top ten," but only 218 for women (total occurrences of all names for men is 2625, for women only 328). That is, the database of male names is a full eight times the size of that for females. Ossuary references make up only 411 total references for the top ten (out of only about 250 such inscriptions—that is, just as in the ossuaries we have been examining, many contained more than one name. Judah, son of Joshua, would count as two names on one inscription). It is interesting to note that the ossuary percentages and the literature percentages are fairly close to one another as well. As we look over the data we might note a few things:

- The combination of Simon and Joseph accounts for nearly 20% of the total, meaning almost one out of five bore one of the two most popular names.

- The combination of Mary and Salome accounts for nearly 40% of the total, meaning almost two out of five bore one of the two most popular names (which surely would have resulted in a perfusion of nicknames/variants on the name).

- The top ten male names account for almost exactly half of the total occurrences.

- The top ten female names account for exactly two thirds of the total occurrences.

- 7.9% of men, and 9.6% of women bore a name found only once in our sources.[94]

The final point should be kept in mind each time you hear the promoters of the tomb theory emphasizing how "unique" Mariamne[95] is, or how "Jose" has only been found once, etc.

Many in modern times struggle to realize that during this time, had you called out either the name Mary or the name Salome in the marketplace, an amazing percentage of the women—over a third—would turn in response. Personally, I had always wondered at the number of Mary's referred to in the Gospels. Now I realize the New Testament is representing the very historical context in which it was birthed and which it accurately reflects.

---

[94] Ibid., 71-72.

[95] Of course, more to the point is the better reading of the inscription in the first place.

Notice as well that Mara is listed separately from Martha, though it may well be that this should be combined with Martha as its diminutive, just as Joses is combined with Joseph. If this was done, Martha/Mara would be the third most popular name.

Let us remember the names in the Talpiot tomb: Jesus (2x), Joseph (2x, including Jose as a form of Joses), Matthew, Judah, and Mary (2x, in different forms), Mara or Martha. *Every single name is found in the top ten of the most common names history records at that time in that place.* It is no wonder the archaeologists viewed them as common names and did not send out press releases to announce the finding of the tomb of Jesus of Nazareth. They had no reason to think so then, and we continue to have no reason to think differently today.

Patina, Knights Templar, and Twins

The arguments from the ossuaries, *The Acts of Philip*, DNA, and statistics are the only semi-substantive portion of the theory propounded in *The Lost Tomb of Jesus* film and book. But there are a few other odd claims made that should be addressed just to provide a response so that no one's mind may be troubled by them. Specifically, much time was spent seeking to put the "James, son of Joseph, brother of Jesus" ossuary into the Talpiot tomb so as to in essence "seal the deal". Next, we have speculation presented regarding the chevron symbol and the Knights Templar, similar to what you have in *The Da Vinci Code*. And finally we have the highly unusual speculation concerning Judah, son of Jesus, being the author of the second-century *Gospel of Thomas*.

Patina and the Suffolk County Crime Lab

Given that at the time of this writing a legal proceeding is ongoing in the state of Israel regarding the famous "James, brother of Jesus" ossuary, we will not invest a great deal of time in the subject here. To say that the provenance and legitimacy of the ossuary is in question would be to state the obvious. We surely shall not solve the issue in our brief discussion. It should be remembered that Simcha Jacobovici, the prime mover in the film and book, has a strong reason to press the legitimacy of the James ossuary. He produced the documentary on the subject for the Discovery Channel. He is on record supporting its authenticity. So by tying the ossuary in to the Talpiot tomb, not only would the James ossuary be shown legitimate, but the "Jesus family tomb" identification would be greatly strengthened. As Pellegrino stated:

"Adding James to the cluster would send the statistics into the stratosphere," I said. "There'd be no question that this is the Jesus family tomb."[96]

But rather than delving into the James issue, I wish to address the claim that the analysis of the patina, the layer of debris, minerals, etc. that develops over time on an object in a tomb, "matches" the James ossuary to the Talpiot tomb.

The spectral analysis of the patina detects relative concentrations of various minerals and chemical compounds in the patina. The analysis indicated that there was a close consistency between the patina in the Talpiot tomb and that on the James ossuary. However, and this is key, all that proves is similarity, not identity. Patina from similar tombs (like the one found just north of the Talpiot tomb) where *terra rosa* had entered the tomb around the same time would be needed for a meaningful comparison, and that kind of study simply was not done. As Robert Genna, Suffolk Co. Crime Laboratory Director wrote in an e-mail to Ted Koppel:

> The elemental composition of some of the samples we tested from the ossuaries are consistent with each other. But I would never say they're a match....No scientist would ever say definitively that one ossuary comes from the same tomb as another...We didn't do enough sampling to see if in fact there were other tombs that had similar elemental compositions...The only samples we can positively say are a 'match' from a single source are fingerprints and DNA.

So while the discussion of the James ossuary allowed the filmmakers to add yet another "science/CSI" connection, in reality, they once again went beyond the actual conclusions of science itself when the narrator intoned the word "match" in reference to the patina analysis. While this information may have relevance to the continued examination of the James ossuary, given the collapse of the argumentation already documented, even placing it in the Talpiot tomb, given the data as we have it right now, would only once again point us to the common nature of the names in the tomb, since James (Jacob) is either the tenth or eleventh most common name, depending on how you run the figures.

---

[96] *TFTJ*, 92.

Dan Brown Redux: The Knights Templar

Certain groups in history are always rife for a new conspiracy theory. The Knights Templar seem to be at the top of the list when it comes to spawning conspiracy theories. They figured prominently in the recreations in Dan Brown's *The Da Vinci Code,* and lo and behold, they show up again in *The Jesus Family Tomb.* This time they aren't defending the royal bloodline, they are beating up on poor Judeo-Christians and finding the Talpiot tomb! And they somehow figured out the inscriptions and what it all meant and were holding this over the Pope's head! Here's how the book spun the story.

Somehow, without providing any expert testimony, with no references to even check, the book determines who broke into the Talpiot tomb and when. We are told this happened in the twelfth century, but we are given no factual basis upon which to even respond to the assertion. Then:

> The intruders opened the seal of the fifth ossuary niche, removed the northernmost ossuary, studied it, and pushed it gently back into place but with one end still protruding. All the ossuaries survived without any signs of being damaged or looted.
>
> In the center of the tomb, the *terra rossa* people left a calling card, of sorts. Three skulls were placed in the chamber in an odd and clearly ceremonial configuration.[97]

How do we know these things? We are not told. Mere assertions. Which ossuary was moved? Yeshua bar Yosef? More silence. And given the number of bones found in the tomb, and the eyewitness testimony that children were kicking skulls around the day the tomb was broken open in 1980, how are we to know that there were three skulls in the chamber "in an odd *and clearly ceremonial* configuration?" The fact is, we don't. And what makes the positioning "clearly ceremonial" outside of the desire of the authors to make a vague connection to a theory about the Knights Templar? This kind of "state it as a fact, do not bother substantiating your conclusions" argumentation is only convincing to those who desire to believe.

At this point an extensive amplification of the Ebionite movement, far beyond anything mainline scholarship has ever envisioned, is presented in the book. I confess I do not understand the

---

[97] *TJFT,* 123.

motivations that have brought this particular element of the book into play, but it is not overly important. They posit a long-running, even powerful Ebionite movement in Jerusalem:

> In other words, as long as Jerusalem stood, it was the Nazarenes/Ebionites who called the theological shots in the Jewish Jesus movement, and they seemed indistinguishable from the general Jewish population.[98]

Then the ever-present "look at this really basic shape, let's build an entire theory on it" idea is sprung on the reader, though, thankfully, without some of the esoteric connections drawn in *The Da Vinci Code*. Without direct knowledge of what the builders of the tomb intended, the chevron shape on the face of the Talpiot tomb (very basic in shape) is seen as vitally important and connected to a similar shape (in the film) on one of the ossuaries found in *Dominus Flevit*. I do not claim a bit of expertise in ancient symbology, but there was one thing that was certain. The entire effort invested in trying to make a slight scratch mark on the Yeshua ossuary into a cross was completely out of line. The mark was a "this side forward" mark, matching the lid. It was meant to mark which direction to slide the lid so it would fit. I believe that was what was on the ossuary shown in the film but then connected to the Talpiot tomb (the circle inside it matching all sorts of other such marks on the limestone of the ossuary). Now, identifying something like that as a "this end up" mark will not sell a single book or get you three hours on the Discovery Channel, so it doesn't get mentioned. But if you can attach it to the Knights Templar, well, that sells!

> Today a similar symbol, represented as a complete pyramid (or triangle) enclosing the all-seeing eye of God, can be found in churches and Masonic temples around the world...[99]

It seems to me a huge leap to jump from a circle under a chevron to the "all-seeing eye." This kind of "this looks like this, which looks like this, which proves a connection" kind of thinking is to be found in every conspiracy novel on the market today.

---

[98] *TJFT*, 127.
[99] *TJFT*, 128.

> Could it be, Tabor wondered, that the chevron, like the symbol
> of the fish, was yet another early symbol of Jesus's first
> followers? In the turbulent, anti-Christian times of Nero
> through Vespasian, could this have been a secret Judeo-
> Christian symbol?[100]

The room for speculation in such areas is, of course, endless. As we
have noted, Tabor will even speculate on the musings of Kabbalistic
rabbis from the sixteenth century as to where Jesus was buried. There
simply are no rules, no limits, to this kind of meandering speculation, as
we see in what follows:

> Here's what I think: clearly, if a complete triangle symbolizes
> the Temple, the unfinished triangle symbolizes the Temple that
> was (as Jesus predicted) destined to fall and which was yet to be
> rebuilt." The Third Temple. The Temple of messianic times, of
> the "End of Days."[101]

Sadly, the first-century interpretation of the meaning of "temple" to
Jesus, especially in his own prophetic prediction of his own resurrection,
is dismissed in favor of fanciful theories such as these.

> "Well, let's review the facts." Jim said. "It is a fact that the
> Templar knights were in Jerusalem during the entire century of
> the First Crusade. It is also one of the mysteries of history how
> they accumulated a lot of power and wealth in very little time.
> Many have speculated that they had something on the church.
> Eventually they became too successful—too many kings and
> bishops owed them money. During the near-total extermination
> of the Templars, the church leveled so many accusations against
> the knights that separating fact from rumor and fabrication is an
> intractable problem."[102]

Indeed, almost as intractable as finding a foothold of fact in the
avalanche of speculation and mythology that is the substance of this
fanciful flight with the Templars.

---

[100] *TJFT*, 129.
[101] *TJFT*, 130.
[102] *TJFT*, 131.

What if the accusers had gotten some of it right? What if the Templars, who were involved in the general slaughter of Jews and Muslims during the Crusades, did come across a small group of Ebionites—a surviving branch of the early Jesus movement? ... Perhaps the Templars also took the symbol on the facade back to Europe, accounting for the introduction of the pyramid and the "all-seeing eye"; did they know that Jesus had not bodily ascended to heaven? Did the Church believe that the Templars were in possession of the skull of Jesus of Nazareth?[103]

What if...perhaps...did they? Such argumentation is always quite useful for those looking for something to believe in that differs from the "norm" or the "mainstream." But what do we really learn from this kind of wild, groundless speculation? We do gain an insight into just how far-ranging our authors are in their thinking on this subject. We have already seen that they are willing to jettison the testimony of first century witnesses in favor of fourth-century fictional writings far removed from the original context, so we need not be surprised at this kind of fanciful speculation either.

Judah Writes a Gospel...of Thomas

I thought I had pretty much exhausted the lengths to which Jacobovici and his team could go in unfounded speculation and the weaving of tapestries of fiction, but then I ran into the section on Judah, son of Jesus. Now, I fully understand the emotional appeal contained in the film's depictions of Judah, "son of Jesus." A very innovative way of getting around the critical thinking portion of the mind through emotional manipulation! Very effective indeed. But I simply cannot begin to understand how Jacobovici and his team ended up making the utterly unfounded, credibility-damaging connection between Judah bar Yeshua of the Talpiot tomb and...the author of the Gnostic Gospel of Thomas! But we should allow them to explain:

> "After they killed fathers, they went after their kids," Simcha said. "The Romans didn't mess about. They called Jesus 'King of the Jews.' They mocked his royal lineage. Any surviving son would have been a target. He had to be hidden. That's why we haven't heard of him."

---

[103] *TJFT*, 132-133.

"Personally, Jim, I think he's the 'Beloved Disciple,'" I said.

"Or is he Judah, the brother of Jesus mentioned in Mark? Or, are they all one and the same—'Beloved Disciple,' 'brother,' 'Son,'" I said, looking at Jim and Simcha. "Look at the history of Roman slaughter. The children of a contender were doomed—and yet, siblings were sometimes allowed to survive. When they killed Caligula, they also killed his infant child, but his sisters were spared, and his uncle Claudius even survived to become emperor. So, within Jesus' inner circle, they knew that the Romans would kill the Prophet's child, while a little brother might be granted at least a fighting chance."

"So what you're saying is that Judah, the 'little brother' of Jesus might actually have been the child of Jesus all along," said Jim. "And the key to his survival was for the disciples to say he was really someone else's child."

"It's not impossible," I said. "Remember, even in the Bible it states that Abraham said his wife Sarah was really his sister in order to save himself. Also, according to Eusebius, around fifty years after the Crucifixion, the emperor Domitian hauls two of Judah's grandsons before him because the Romans still feel threatened by the descendants of Jesus."[104]

When you see someone including lines like, "it is not impossible" in the midst of an argument that has started off by precluding the relevance and accuracy of the only records that actually date to the time period in question, you know you have a problem. But more than that, the entire foundation of this conversation has missed the mark. The Romans were not Jesus' primary opponents. The Jewish leaders were. The accusation of being King of the Jews was not because the Romans had seen Jesus as an ever-growing threat. In fact, Pilate saw no reason to crucify him. But the Jewish leaders did, and they pressed for his execution. Our theorists, always willing to take from the New Testament a fact here, a statement there, while rejecting the rest of it out of hand, have missed the entire context of the crucifixion and turned it into solely a Roman activity for some odd reason. There is not a scintilla of foundation for viewing the "beloved disciple" as Judah, as we will see below.

In any case, I know it is bad form to disrupt a "bull session" of harmless speculation (is it really that harmless?) with a sudden insertion of facts, but it has been so long since we have stood upon the solid

---

[104] *TJFT*, 90-91.

ground of actual historical documentation that it might be good to introduce some now. Though no references were provided to the mention of Eusebius, those familiar with the field can track down the actual sources. Here is the actual statement of Eusebius to which Pellegrino made reference:

Chapter 19
But when this same Domitian had commanded that the descendants of David should be slain, an ancient tradition says that some of the heretics brought accusation against the descendants of Jude (said to have been a brother of the Savior according to the flesh), on the ground that they were of the lineage of David and were related to Christ himself. Hegesippus relates these facts in the following words.

Chapter 20
Of the family of the Lord there were still living the grandchildren of Jude, who is said to have been the Lord's brother according to the flesh. Information was given that they belonged to the family of David, and they were brought to the Emperor Domitian by the Evocatus. For Domitian feared the coming of Christ as Herod also had feared it. And he asked them if they were descendants of David, and they confessed that they were. Then he asked them how much property they had, or how much money they owned. And both of them answered that they had only nine thousand denarii, half of which belonged to each of them; and this property did not consist of silver, but of a piece of land which contained only thirty-nine acres, and from which they raised their taxes and supported themselves by their own labor. Then they showed their hands, exhibiting the hardness of their bodies and the callousness produced upon their hands by continuous toil as evidence of their own labor. And when they were asked concerning Christ and his kingdom, of what sort it was and where and when it was to appear, they, answered that it was not a temporal nor an earthly kingdom, but a heavenly and angelic one, which would appear at the end of the world, when he should come in glory to judge the quick and the dead, and to give unto every one according to his works. Upon hearing this, Domitian did not pass judgment against them, but, despising them as of no account, he let them go, and by a decree put a

stop to the persecution of the Church. But when they were released they ruled the churches because they were witnesses and were also relatives of the Lord. And peace being established, they lived until the time of Trajan. These things are related by Hegesippus.[105]

Now note what Eusebius actually says. First, this did not happen because the Romans were afraid of anything. "Certain heretics" brought these charges based upon a command that the sons of David should be killed. If anything, this speaks of an anti-Jewish feeling, possibly related to the frequent insurrections in Palestine. Next, he says that Domitian feared the coming of Christ as Herod had feared it. It does not say he feared a dynasty, nor was he seeking the children of Jesus, etc. He instead inquired concerning the nature of Christ's kingdom, and, upon hearing the same message Jesus had given to Pilate, he, being a good Roman, despised them and released them. Once again, the actual citation does not support the conspiracy theory, so it is much easier to make a passing reference, choose your facts carefully, skip the facts that won't fit, and move on before anyone notices.

> And yet, logically, if Jesus had a wife and son, either they would not have been spoken of at all, or they would have been spoken of in code.[106]

Or, like the rest of the Christian community, including his mother, they would have trusted God with their lives and been open confessors of Jesus Christ.

> In Christian tradition, "Judah" the brother of Jesus comes down to us as St. Jude, one of the Apostles. Another Apostle comes down to us as Judas Thomas Didymos. ..."Didymos" was a word, not a name. Quite literally, and simply, it was the Greek word for "twin." As for "Thomas," no such name has ever existed in Hebrew. This too is a word and not a name. Thomas—"Te-om" in Hebrew—has always meant "twin."[107]

---

[105] Eusebius, *Ecclesiastical History*, III:19-20, in Philip Schaff and Henry Wace, *Nicene and Post-Nicene Fathers of the Christian Church* (2nd Series), (Grand Rapids: Eerdmans, 1982), I:148-149.
[106] *TJFT*, 105.
[107] *TJFT*, 107.

Correct, which is why, in the Gospels,[108] Thomas (Hebrew) is also known as "Didymus" (Greek). Having a Hebrew and Greek version of a name was commonplace. Nowhere is Thomas identified, however, as Jude or Judas. Our writers note that the Gospel of Thomas begins by naming its author as "Didymos Judas Thomas." They then assert:

> The name strongly suggests that Judas (the brother) and Thomas were indeed one and the same person. In the Gospel of Thomas (saying 11), Jesus says to Thomas, "On the day when you were one, you became two." That seems to be exactly what happened to Judas. He became both Judas and Thomas: "Twin Judas Twin."[109]

I confess I cannot even follow this line of reasoning. Is it not much more likely that the author of the Gospel of Thomas, being removed from first-century Palestine by a full century or more, quite possibly removed linguistically as well (he probably did not know Hebrew, and hence would not know the background of Thomas), seeking to promote himself as a purveyor of secret knowledge, simply chose these names as a convenient and useful platform for his book? We know even Judas Iscariot managed to get a neat fictional gospel out of the Gnostics, so asking for specific linguistic meanings from books that contain sayings like "On the day when you were one, you became two" is missing the entire point of the genre of literature. These statements are not meant to be interpreted in this way. The whole point of "secret knowledge" was keeping it secret. But then our theorists leap far out into the unknown when they take this convoluted foundation, and say:

> This strange code would be impossible to break were it not for an ossuary in Talpiot inscribed "Judah, son of Jesus." Can it be that the son became the "twin"—perhaps an ancient code for "junior"—in order to protect him from the Roman authorities? Can it be that Jesus' son has been hiding—touchingly, like a child—in plain sight all along?[110]

---

[108] John specifically records this fact, 11:16, 21:2.
[109] Ibid.
[110] *TJFT*, 108.

The Talpiot tomb breaks the code of the Gospel of Thomas written a full century after the tomb was sealed? And that on the basis of "can it be" and "perhaps"? This kind of reasoning is so torturous and circular that it defies logical refutation. But it only gets worse:

> At the Last Supper, in the Gospel of John, the Beloved Disciple is depicted as "leaning against Jesus' chest." Again, sticking to the plain meaning of the text, what does it tell us about this "beloved" male? Unless your eating habits are very different from mine, at my dinner table only my kids cuddle with me and lean against my chest. The Beloved Disciple, therefore, is clearly very young. He's not a baby or a toddler, but he is also not a full-grown man. He's a kid, a young boy. This interpretation is not new. In fact, Albrecht Dürer, the famous German painter, in his masterful depiction of the Last Supper on a woodcut, has a young boy sitting in Jesus' lap. Simply put, it's what the text says.[111]

The problem here of course lies in the fact that our writers seem ignorant of how meals were taken in first-century Israel. They make the same error made by medieval painters and assume that they used tables and chairs, and hence anyone lying on Jesus' chest would have to be adopting an unusual position. But it is well-known that meals were taken lying down, which is why, for example, when the woman anoints Jesus' feet while he is reclining at the table, she is able to do so without crawling under anyone to get there! Jesus' head would be inward, toward the table, and his feet away from the table, accessible in that way. One would in essence lie on one side, propped up with cushions, or simply one's elbows, to eat. Now the picture is easily understood as to the beloved disciple leaning upon Jesus' chest: he is the closest one to Jesus, toward whom Jesus is facing. To speak to him, especially in private, would be fairly easy to do, but would involve leaning inward toward each other. It is truly amazing to read such a basic error in a book that speaks so much about ancient archaeology!

Finally, as if to communicate as clearly as possible the utter unreliability of the New Testament text one last time, our authors redefine the scene recorded in John 19:25-27:

---

[111] *TJFT*, 207.

> 25 Therefore the soldiers did these things. But standing by the cross of Jesus were His mother, and His mother's sister, Mary the *wife* of Clopas, and Mary Magdalene. 26 When Jesus then saw His mother, and the disciple whom He loved standing nearby, He said to His mother, "Woman, behold, your son!" 27 Then He said to the disciple, "Behold, your mother!" From that hour the disciple took her into his own *household.*

Please note: there are soldiers present at the cross. Likewise, Jesus' mother and others are present, including Mary Magdalene. When Jesus sees his mother Mary, he speaks to the same disciple who, along with the other disciples, had shared dinner with him only a matter of hours before, and that disciple takes her into his household from that time onward. This is a man, for he has a household. He is John, the author of this Gospel. He is not "Judah bar Yeshua" of the Talpiot tomb. Yet, nothing is beyond the reach of the speculation of the tomb theorists:

> Furthermore, John records that Jesus saw his mother with the Beloved Disciple at the foot of the cross. He then says to her: "Woman, behold thy son!" Turning to the Beloved Disciple, he states: "Behold thy mother!" (John 19:26–27). From then on, John tells us, Mary shared the same home as the Beloved Disciple. Clearly, they're family. Most probably, grandmother and grandson.
>
> Alternatively, isn't it possible, as some scholars have suggested, that Mary Magdalene is often replaced in the Gospels by Mary, mother of Jesus, in order to obscure her role in Jesus' life? If this is the case, the incident at the cross can be reinterpreted as a dying man's last words to his wife ("woman"), not his mother, asking her to overcome her grief and protect their son from imminent danger.[112]

Clearly they are family? Then why did Jesus even have to say these words? The real reason is easy to see: Mary is alone, family-wise, at the cross. Jesus' brothers are, at this time, unbelievers. He entrusts his mother to the one closest to him, and this one takes her into his home from that point onward. To even speculate otherwise is to make a mockery of the situation, for if this was Mary's grandson, *his duties would already be well-known to him.* But as if this absurd rewriting of the text

---

112 *TJFT*, 208-209.

based upon groundless speculation were not enough, now a whole new scenario is proposed, one that turns Mary into Mary Magdalene (though John noted her presence as well). Here we are told that though the family was deathly afraid of the Romans, here, in front of Roman guards, Jesus points out his wife and son! The length to which these writers will go to propose *anything* other than what is found in the Gospel texts is truly a sight to behold.

James Cameron's View of Christianity

He is known as one of the most successful directors in the industry today, and deservedly so. James Cameron has likewise shown a great interest in the exploration of Mars, for example, and has contributed toward the design of spacecraft. So one would expect that before putting pen to paper and publishing statements on something as widely discussed and understood as the form and history of the Christian faith that the same kind of care would be taken in accurately representing the topics at hand.

Unfortunately, such is not the case, as documented by Cameron's Foreword to *The Family Tomb of Jesus.*[113] Instead, Cameron's Foreword gives us an invaluable insight into the mindset of many in our culture today, a mindset that accepts the worst scholarship has to offer as a given, and does not provide the first opportunity for historic Christianity to offer a response. While Mr. Cameron has disavowed theological expertise, it should be noted that he has directed a film that, as we have already seen, is theological to its core. And the comments he makes in his foreword, stating fictions as facts, shows just how much work must be done to speak the truth in a culture more than happy to believe the worst about Christianity whenever possible.

James Cameron did not take long to get to the ravaging of the historic Christian faith:

> In various pagan mystery religions predating the first century C.E. (A.D.), Osiris, Attis, and Dionysus were all god-men who died around the time of Easter (the spring equinox) and were resurrected after three days. And all three of these deities

---

[113] *TJFT*, vii – xiv.

predated Jesus by centuries. Christmas itself is thought by most scholars to be an adoption of the pagan tradition of celebrating the winter solstice. With many of the basic narrative points of the Jesus story, such as the virgin birth and the Resurrection, predating his supposed existence by hundreds of years, a compelling case has been made that he never existed at all but was a myth created to fulfill a specific need. In the absence of a single particle of physical evidence that Jesus Christ actually lived, this recent movement among historical scholars could not be factually refuted.[114]

While it is very common to hear the allegations concerning Osiris, Attis, and Dionysus repeated by certain extremists on the left, one could hope that Cameron would show a bit more insight. To call this statement "false" is to be kind to it. It is simply untenable on any level. The number of logical disconnections between *any* of the stories referred to by Cameron would take another book to document. But since Cameron's comment is so often repeated by others in our cultural context, let's note a few facts.

First, none of the religions mentioned (Egyptian paganism in the case of Osiris, Greek mythology in the case of Dionysus and Attis), were monotheistic religions with a single creator God, maker of all things. While some may not see the relevance, to the student of religion, the starting place is quite important. The myths and stories of these religions were subject to major revision and change depending on location, *and this was considered normal.* The view of history in these religions is completely different from that of the Christian faith.

But beyond these foundational differences, the idea that any of these gods represent a resurrection even slightly similar to that claimed by the Christian faith is just outrageous on its face. For example, Dionysus. Did he die and rise again in three days around Easter? Surely not. Instead, the "resurrection" connection is found in the story of his birth. In one version, when Zeus appears, his glory kills Dionysus' mother Semele, so Zeus rescues the fetal Dionysus *and sews him in his thigh.* Dionysus' "resurrection" is to come forth from Zeus' thigh! I suppose it is possible someone could be so completely ignorant of the Christian scriptures as to think there is some kind of a parallel between the resurrection of Christ from the dead and the birth of a baby who was sewn into Zeus' thigh, but it is hard to imagine. In another version

---

[114] *TJFT*, vii.

of the Dionysus story, his mother is not Semele, but Persephone. In this story, the baby is born but lured away by Titans who chop him up and eat everything but his heart, which Zeus then uses to recreate him in the womb of Semele. In some versions, she eats the heart and thus becomes pregnant. In any case, the idea that Dionysus is a parallel to Jesus is, of course, absurd on its face, at least when the facts are allowed to speak for themselves.

Likewise the Osiris myth provides no meaningful connection to the resurrection of Christ either. There are many versions of the story, differing from one another in many details. In the most popular version, Osiris' brother Set traps him in a coffin and throws him in the Nile. Isis, his wife, found his body in Byblos and brought it back to Egypt. But Set found the body and tore it into pieces (some versions say 14 parts), throwing the parts in the Nile. Isis once again finds almost all the parts, or at least almost all of them (I am skipping over the explicit portions of the pagan myth), bandages them together (making the first mummy), and he travels to the underworld where he becomes the king there in a somewhat zombified state. There is no resurrection in the Christian context to be found here, and the date of Osiris' festival (November 13th) does not connect as claimed by Cameron. Strike two.

This leaves us with Attis. According to Greek mythology, a daemon named Agdistis was distrusted by the Olympian gods, who castrated him and threw the organ away. But from it grew an almond tree. When the fruit of the almond tree became ripe, a woman named Nana placed it on her bosom. The fruit disappeared, and she became pregnant. Her child was Attis. Then, when Attis was to marry, Cybele appeared in great power, driving him mad, causing him to castrate himself. For some reason, his wife-to-be's father-in-law followed suit, leading to the basis for the "Corybantes," followers of Cybele who likewise castrated themselves. Attis himself died but was reborn...as an evergreen pine. Once again, to even suggest a meaningful parallel, let alone the idea that the story of Christ is based upon such pagan myths, requires a level of credulity far beyond anything I can possibly manage. Believing something like that would be similar to believing fourth-century ascetic vegetarians are a better source of historical information on the life of Jesus than the Apostles themselves! And surely, no one would ever do that, would they?

Mr. Cameron thinks that a "compelling case" has been made that Jesus never existed. He must be thinking of such presentations as those made by radical skeptics like Robert Price in his *Deconstructing Jesus*[115] or *The Incredible Shrinking Son of Man*.[116]   But to find such ransacking of history for any reason to disbelieve "compelling" requires a pretty radical starting point in one's own thinking, to be sure. Of course, no such "compelling" case has ever been set forth that does not partake of the most egregious violations of consistency and appropriate historical methodology, and Cameron's repetition of the Osiris/Attis/Dionysus/whoever-else statement is good indication that what he finds "compelling" in these matters is not what a serious historian or theologian would find compelling.

> This book chronicles a three-year investigation of the most stunning archaeological find of the last century. With systematic rigor, Simcha and Charlie analyze the physical evidence, cross-referencing it with clues from both the canonical and the apocryphal Gospels to fill in the first complete picture of the Jesus family. It reads like a gripping detective novel, and one has to pinch oneself to remember that it is real. Absolutely real.[117]

The Talpiot tomb is real. The ossuaries are real. The inscriptions (however one reads them) are real. The Encratite community of Asia Minor was real. Mitochondrial DNA is real. No question about any of these things. But it is how you relate these things to one another that determines if, in fact, any of your *conclusions* are real, and as we have seen, those promoting this theory have shown a stunning willingness to see what they want to see, and not see what is far more obvious. The "systematic rigor" was only detectable in the systematic spinning of data so as to come to a particular conclusion. The standards applied to the canonical Gospels are completely other than those applied to the Gnostics, for example. The "rigor" applied to the DNA was to see in it a marriage that DNA can never, ever prove or even address. There was indeed a systematic element to the book, but it was a systematic abuse of the canons of scholarship so as to produce what the authors just "knew" had to be there.

---

[115] Robert M. Price, *Deconstructing Jesus* (Amherst, NY: Prometheus Books, 2000).
[116] Robert M. Price, *The Incredible Shrinking Son of Man* (Amherst, NY: Prometheus Books, 2003).
[117] *TJFT*, viii.

> One and a half billion Christians—more than one-fifth of the world's population—believe they know exactly who Jesus was. But what do we really know for sure?[118]

Evidently, while we can know for certain that dead bodies chopped into fourteen pieces in Egypt and turned into zombies in an afterlife is a parallel to Jesus' resurrection, we cannot know what the Gospels, written in the first century by the first and second generations of the followers of Jesus, actually reveal about Christ. The double standard is not new with Cameron, of course. He is imbibing it uncritically from his sources, but that does not change the fact that it is a double standard.

> Until now, there has been zero physical evidence of his existence. No fingerprints, no bones, no portraits done from life, nothing. Not a shred of parchment written in Jesus's own hand,[119]

If we followed the historical paradigm introduced here we would question the existence of just about everyone who ever lived prior to the printing press. Fingerprints? Bones? Portraits? This is the evidence of ancient history? One is truly left breathless at the breadth of the claims inherent in such statements, and how far from reality they would take us.

> Most of what we know, or think we know, comes from the four great Gospels of Matthew, Mark, Luke, and John. But what exactly are these Gospels? To the deeply and unquestioningly faithful, they are the direct and absolute word of God, recorded by the most saintly of men. Historians, however, now view them as composite works, each created by several authors and based in turn on oral traditions carried on for decades, possibly half a century, after Christ's actual ministry. There is no historical evidence that any of the authors, if in fact they were individuals, actually heard the words of Jesus from his own lips.[120]

---

[118] *TJFT*, viii.
[119] Ibid.
[120] *TJFT*, ix.

Notice how to be deeply faithful is to be unquestioningly faithful. How does that follow? We are not told, of course, because it is untrue. One can be quite widely read and deeply concerned about historical issues, etc. and still deeply faithful. We are also told these Gospels were written by the "most saintly of men." Really? The authority of the Gospels is not based upon the men who wrote them. That should be fairly obvious because some, like Matthew, *are anonymous in the first place.* If the author was the issue, they would make much of his name, etc.

Next, notice that in Cameron's mind, there is a complete disjunction between "the faithful" and "historians." Evidently, he is unaware of the existence of *faithful historians,* or historians who recognize the historical value and credibility of the Gospels. His view of the Gospels is quite common, but he shows no evidence of knowing of the existence of such monumental works as Bauckham's *Jesus and the Eyewitnesses*[121] or any number of other works demonstrating the accuracy and reliability of the Gospels. It would be good for Mr. Cameron to familiarize himself with the literature of the field before making sweeping statements about there being "no evidence." But beyond this, it is ironic to find this kind of observation about the Gospels in the foreword to a book that promotes *The Acts of Philip* as a reliable historic source. Cameron clearly accepts *The Acts of Philip* as reliable, yet one is truly forced to wonder if he has even *read* the work. And if so, does he apply the same historically skeptical criteria to it that he does to the Gospels? If not, why not?

Cameron's historiography is surely one that would not yield much in the way of scholarly consensus:

> As a result of this twelve-year investigation (relating to the Titanic), I have come to realize that history is a consensus hallucination. It is a myth upon which we all agree to agree. The truth is a moving target: new evidence must always be weighed, and "the truth" updated. Historical records must always be questioned, and the agenda or perceptual context of those doing the recording must always be considered.[122]

I wonder why the "agenda" or "perceptual context" of the Encratite community in Asia Minor did not figure in Cameron's thinking in the

---

121 Richard Bauckham, *Jesus and the Eyewitnesses: The Gospels as Eyewitness Testimony.* (Grand Rapids: Eerdmans, 2006).
122 *TJFT,* ix – x.

production of this film?   Now that he knows that both Carney Matheson and Francois Bovon have indicated that they were taken out of context by Simcha Jacobovici, will he amend and change his views on the topic, in light of the clear "agenda" that has been documented? Only time can tell.

> The story that Simcha and Charlie tell of the Jesus family tomb is pieced together from hard physical evidence, evidence that cannot lie. It simply is what it is. But the physical evidence must nevertheless be interpreted in a historical context, and that interpretation depends heavily on the sparse details about Jesus and his family that can be gleaned from historical sources. How does the new evidence support or contradict what the historical record has been telling us for two millennia?[123]

No, as Gill Grissom would definitely agree, evidence cannot lie. But those handling the evidence can spin it; they can ignore other readings of how one piece of evidence relates to another, etc. But it is naïve in the extreme to say that evidence "simply is what it is." For example, the inscriptions must be interpreted, and, if this had been done in a truly scholarly context, there would have been much discussion over whether "Mariamne" is even a valid reading of the ossuary to begin with. And the DNA evidence "is what it is," but if you inaccurately expand its purview so that it speaks to relationships that it simply cannot establish, you can no longer speak of it as "hard" evidence. Now it has become nothing but spin.

> The Gospels as we know them today have been retranscribed and rewritten many times and translated from one language to another—from Aramaic to Greek to Coptic to Latin to various forms of English—with corresponding losses in nuanced meaning. They have been edited by Church fathers, centuries after the original words were spoken, to conform to their subsequent vision of orthodoxy. And yet, in the absence of the tiniest scrap of concrete physical evidence, they were our only record of the life and times of Jesus.[124]

---

[123] *TJFT*, x.
[124] *TJFT*, x.

Here we have a real opportunity to test Mr. Cameron's knowledge of the facts, and he fails the test miserably. It honestly seems as if he thinks the biblical text has come down to us in the "phone game" format, translated from one language to another, "with corresponding losses in nuanced meaning." Is it possible he is ignorant of the fact that English Bible translations today are translated directly from Hebrew and Greek? Does he not know that Christian scholars translate from the originals daily? Then we have the bald assertion of "editing by Church fathers." No evidence is provided, but might he be relying upon the likes of Bart Ehrman?[125] It is difficult to respond to such sweeping accusations, but suffice it to say that the depth and breadth of the New Testament manuscript tradition provides us with the ability to detect any attempt at modifying the original message of the texts themselves. Just the opposite is true for the key text utilized by Cameron and his compatriots in the tomb story, *The Acts of Philip*. Its text is hopelessly corrupt and testified to at the earliest by a manuscript a thousand years removed from the original. In comparison to the state of the text of *The Acts of Philip*, the two most widely divergent texts of the New Testament would look like carbon copies of each other! Once again, the double standard is very easy to detect.

> Complicating matters are the other Gospels: the apocryphal texts such as the Gnostic Gospels of the Nag Hammadi Library found in the Egyptian desert in 1945. Buried in an earthen jar to keep them from the Christian orthodoxy of the fourth century, which sought to eradicate all the so-called heresies, these precious and astonishing books show the rich diversity of early Christian thought and give clues to the historical story not available in the Big Four of Matthew, Mark, Luke, and John.[126]

Those horrible "orthodox" Christians of the fourth century! I mean, into the second decade of that century they were still being persecuted by the Roman Empire, and the Romans were doing all they could to eradicate the Christians and their Scriptures, but they still somehow managed to "eradicate" all heresies! I get the feeling Mr. Cameron does not believe there is anything like a "heresy," that Christians should just allow every perversion of their faith to go unchallenged. In any case, do we see the same kind of skepticism Cameron aimed at the Gospels

---

[125] Bart Ehrman, *The Orthodox Corruption of Scripture* (Oxford, 1993).
[126] *TJFT*, x.

(which clearly were written in the first century, and which, despite Cameron's earlier remarks, do contain eyewitness testimony) applied to the second and third-century Gnostic writings? If he were to be consistent, he would have to dismiss them as next to irrelevant if he applied the same standards. But instead, we see that they are "precious and astonishing books." Precious and astonishing? I have certainly used the term "astonishing" of them myself, but mainly in the context of being astonished that anyone would find in these fictional works anything even slightly close to the testimony found in the canonical Gospels. Just how do these works give "clues" to the "historical story"? We are not told. It is just assumed, much as it is just assumed that the most skeptical views of the Gospels are correct as well.

> In the Gospel of Mary and the Acts of Philip, for example, Mary Magdalene is known as the "Apostle to the Apostles," an important teacher and partner in Jesus' ministry whom Jesus favored even over Simon Peter. She is described as Jesus' "companion," and she even kissed him on his "mouth" (the word many supply for what is a missing word in the Gospel), to the chagrin of the other disciples. What was this all about? Magdalene is a cryptic figure in the canonical Gospels: mentioned more than any other woman except Jesus' mother, Mary, she is present at both the Crucifixion and the Resurrection. Why is she so important?[127]

Of course, Cameron is now writing his own fiction, for there is no Mary Magdalene in *The Acts of Philip*. None. Mariamne, according to Bovon, is a literary parallel to the Gnostic Magdalene, but there is no historical connection between these two fictional literary devices. Cameron is simply repeating the ancient Gnostic party line, not realizing that by doing so he is placing himself firmly in the camp of those who, 1,740 years ago, were willing to create fictional characters to substantiate their theologies. The irony here is parallel to that which appeared last year during *The Da Vinci Code* episode. Dan Brown turned the Gnostics into the orthodox of the day, but he did so at the expense of turning their actual beliefs on their head. Brown alleged Constantine created the idea of the deity of Christ out of whole cloth and suppressed the Gnostic gospels which presented a very human Jesus. Just the opposite is the case. While the Jesus of Gnosticism does at times engage in evil sexual

---

[127] *TJFT*, x – xi.

activities, he was likewise a heavenly, resurrected being, quite disconnected from any true humanity. It is the canonical Gospels of the first century that present the Jesus who hungered, thirsted, and grew tired on the road through Samaria. But they likewise give not a hint of a married Jesus, let alone that Mary Magdalene was his wife, and so later generations fictionalized the story. And while it is true Mary Magdalene is mentioned "more often," as we have seen, that is a misleading statement. More often, in comparison to almost no references by name to anyone else, is hardly a relevant statement. And when Luke does mention her earlier in his gospel, as one who experienced healing at Jesus' hand, he likewise closes the door on the very Mary Magdalene/Mariamne connection Cameron and Jacobovici rely upon!

> Through both brilliant scholarly research and forensic lab work, Simcha and Charlie answer that question resoundingly....The conclusions he and Simcha are able to draw are virtually irrefutable, and yet they are stunning in their implications.[128]

Virtually irrefutable? We have seen the conclusions are virtually unsubstantiatable, let alone irrefutable! A long string of highly doubtful assertions that are presented without even allowing for far more reasonable reading of the same data is hardly an "irrefutable" argument! I am sorry, but when Mr. Cameron views this work as "brilliant scholarly research," I simply turn to the book and cite Jacobovici and Pellegrino:

> As recorded in the Gospel of Thomas, Simon and Peter, in sayings 22 and 114, eventually rose and spoke out against Mary Magdalene. Declaring that a woman was not worthy of spirit-life, the two men demanded that Mary be ejected from the congregation.[129]

There is nothing about Mary Magdalene, or Simon Peter, in saying 22 of the *Gospel of Thomas*. And in 114 (which is probably a later addition), it is Simon Peter (one man), not Simon *and* Peter (two men), as presented in the book. This kind of basic, simplistic error is the norm, not the exception, in the scholarship of the work.

---

[128] *TJFT*, xi.
[129] *TJFT*, 98.

Our society has a schizophrenic relationship to the concept of empirical proof. We rely on a complex science of criminal forensics in our justice system. We use advanced instrumentation to analyze minute samples of blood, fiber, and DNA evidence, all with the purpose of determining the fate of individuals, sometimes with life-or-death consequences. And yet, according to recent polls, 45 percent of Americans don't believe in evolution. Almost half of this rational, show-me-the-proof society is capable of ignoring two hundred years of scientific investigation—science performed with the same rigor and the same instrumentation used to judge a man's life.

Or, unlike Cameron, some of us *have* studied that data and have concluded that the complexity of the DNA molecule and the mechanism used to decode it is far beyond the realm of naturalistic explanations? Possibly we have come to recognize that the biochemical reactions in the eye that allow you to read the symbols on this page defy any naturalistic explanation as to how they arose? Obviously Cameron is a good, consistent naturalistic materialist in his worldview, but that does not make his conclusions follow logically from the facts.

> We had to use proper control groups to eliminate false posi-tives. We had to enlist the aid of impartial and well-credentialed researchers to perform the forensic and statistical analyses. And we had to have a period of peer review to vet our conclusions, just as we would do with a scientific paper.[130]

This is exactly what did *not* happen, as we have demonstrated. If it had, the very credentialed scholars they utilized would not now be busy sending out e-mails demonstrating how they were taken out of context! This project was kept under wraps (the constant references to confidentiality contracts proves this) and was *not* exposed to the rigors of scholarly examination, and that's the problem.

Finally, in the Discovery Channel interview with Cameron, he comments:

> Faith and forensics make very uneasy bedfellows because to the truly faithful there's no need for evidence, I mean faith implies essentially the lack of a need for evidence. You don't have to

---

[130] *TJFT*, xiii.

prove it to somebody, they believe it from within, through God's grace or whatever. The scientific method is in direct opposition to that. The scientific method says, 'Never assume that what you see is what it is.' You know, that you have to investigate and you have to find the proof, the data, and all that.

Cameron admits to no theological training, and yet, he saw fit to make a good number of comments on theological issues. Here he misdefines faith (at least Christian faith). Faith is placed in the promises of God, and it transcends the merely physical plane, but it is not opposed to evidence or truth. This is a very common, and very improper, view of "religion and science." Cameron thinks the two are in contradiction to each other, but this only proves that he is completely unfamiliar with the Christian worldview and the biblical view of science.

Cameron's comments give us an insight into the mind-set that produced *The Lost Tomb of Jesus*. An imbalanced view of nature and science (naturalistic materialism), combined with a completely undiscerning view of history and the Bible, has led to the results we have documented in this book. It is surely our hope that this failed foray into the theological realm will result in Mr. Cameron's reappraisal of his beliefs and a willingness on his part to hear the other side.

The Road to Emmaus

It is a long way from Toronto to Emmaus, both on a map and in the world of thought as well. Skeptics are quite comfortable staying in Toronto. They do not see any reason at all to walk down the road toward Emmaus. "It's such a long walk, after all, and we are quite happy where we are," they say.

One of those skeptics is James Tabor. In 2006 he put out a book, *The Jesus Dynasty.*[131] As you read the book you come to recognize the genre of academic skepticism that is expressing itself in literally dozens of titles each year pouring forth from Harper San Francisco and Simon and Schuster, etc. The outline is always the same. The first and foundational assumption of all of these books is, "Whatever the truth of the matter, one thing must always be affirmed: Christianity, especially in its dogmatic, historical formulations, must be wrong. Period. Everything else is fair game." To assist in promulgating this viewpoint, any historical source, no matter how outrageous its provenance, how disconnected it might be to the actual events of Jesus or the early church, is elevated to the highest level of authority. Witness the attitude of many today toward anything associated with Gnosticism, such as *The Gospel of Thomas.* The new Gnostic academics approach these texts with the same awe and religious adoration Christians display toward the Bible itself. So, they join the elevation of these texts with the denigration of the biblical texts, and the result is that each writer, whether it be Tabor, or Price, or Borg, or Crossan or any other number of others, produces a "new" picture of Jesus. Of course, each picture contradicts that of the others, so one is left with the impression that there really is no way to know anything about this Jesus fellow anyway, "and the scholars have

---

[131] James Tabor, *The Jesus Dynasty: The Hidden History of Jesus, His Royal Family, and the Birth of Christianity.* New York: Simon and Schuster, 2006.

proven it to be so." And with the imprimatur of "scholarship," the case is closed.

James Tabor, for example, is able to put out a book in 2006 that contains a number of pages of discussion of the Talpiot tomb, yet it likewise suggests a spot in Galilee as the final resting place of Jesus (since he could not have risen from the dead, something he dismisses as "magical" in the film), and even includes a picture of him kneeling over the grave.[132] In a matter of months he is on the *Discovery Channel* providing Jacobovici with thin scholastic cover for his Talpiot theory. It really does not matter, it seems, where you put the grave of Jesus, *just as long as you keep him dead.* I have the feeling that we have not seen the last of DNA/statistics arguments seeking to make their mark and earn their slice of the pie in the "Jesus market."

The serious-minded reader has to ask him or herself a basic question: what would cause otherwise rational, intelligent men and women to invest authority and trust in a textually uncertain, fictionalized, late work like *The Acts of Philip*, while at the very same time rejecting as hopelessly corrupt the documents of the New Testament, which in contrast are the best attested written documents of antiquity and are clearly directly connected to the first century? What would cause them to "hear" Carney Matheson's DNA analysis in such a fashion as to miss something as major as "maternal relationships only"? What could cause them to desire to find Mary Magdalene in *any* historical source so that they could confuse literary parallels with historical realities (in the words of Francois Bovon)? And how could the authors repeatedly speak of Jesus of Nazareth and seemingly not even hear the word "Nazareth," let alone ponder what it means? How could they turn the Jordan River into Jerusalem? Were these men just extremely careless and sloppy, or is there another reason for this kind of consistent behavior?

An Argument Not Considered

There is an argument that was noted briefly in the text but not expanded upon. I consider it fatal to the Talpiot theory but did not wish to have its weight diminished by including it only in passing while examining the arguments presented in the film and the book.

The Jewish leadership of Jerusalem was comprised of a powerful group of men who protected their power as jealously as any ever have. Though Jacobovici and his crew seek to minimize their role in the

---

[132] Tabor, *The Jesus Dynasty*, pp. 238-239.

events of the death of Christ, the New Testament and simple logic will not allow them. They had managed to keep their Temple and their positions of authority through the turbulent years of Roman rule in Palestine, so they were obviously skilled in the political realm. They knew everyone who lived in Jerusalem and carefully monitored the political scene and balance of power. Every time Jesus came to Jerusalem, they not only knew of his arrival, they surely knew about it before he got there. They had informants throughout Judea and Galilee.

In light of this, it is simply unthinkable that Jesus could dwell in Jerusalem as a citizen, obtain a house, establish a family, and have children outside of the Jewish leadership's knowledge. And can you imagine how often his marriage to a woman who had been demonized would be raised as an objection to his criticisms of their leadership and their lifestyle? Their every action would be watched and scrutinized. And after the crucifixion, a squad of Roman soldiers would be on the doorstep of the home in no time, address promptly provided by those who had only a bit earlier been yelling, "Crucify! Crucify!"

But more directly to the point of the Talpiot theory is the fact that, had there existed a multi-generational tomb in the environs of Jerusalem, a "Jesus family tomb," its location and identity would have been well known to the Jewish leadership. The workers who constructed it, those living in the area, would all have known of its existence. It could not have been a secret. And this simple fact presents an insurmountable objection to the Talpiot myth.

The greatest single apologetic argument that could ever be raised against the Christian faith in those early decades would have been the identity and location of the bones of Jesus Christ. The Sanhedrin would have set up daily tours of the Talpiot tomb replete with signs and placards indicating whose bones were on display. And the infant Christian church would have never come into existence. Remember, the New Testament records that representatives of the Jewish leadership followed Paul all the way to Rome. Since the resurrection of Christ was central to his message, the existence of Jesus' bones would have been insurmountable refutation of his message.

But, of course, the Jews never set up tours of the Talpiot tomb. Oh surely they would have known of this tomb and the generations of the family sealed inside it waiting for that day in March of 1980 when the sun burst into its recesses for the first time in many centuries. That is because the family to whom it belonged lived in Jerusalem. The Yeshua whose ossuary has become the focus of so much attention would have been known to history as *Jesus of Jerusalem*, not Jesus of

Nazareth. But there was no connection between this Yeshua, son of Joseph, and the Jesus of Nazareth who created such a stir at the beginning of the fourth decade of the first century. I imagine this Yeshua would find the ruckus raised over his ossuary quite offensive, to be sure.

The reality of the situation in Jerusalem in those decades prior to its destruction by Titus and the Roman legions in A.D. 70 makes the entire Talpiot theory untenable, and the documentation provided in this book only serves to lay the theory to a final and merciful rest.

Trying to Fill an Empty Tomb

It is not possible to be neutral about Jesus of Nazareth. Many make the attempt today, but it simply won't work. His words, his teachings, his claims, are just too radical. They leave you no place to hide. In a politically correct world, he was anything but. He spoke of truth, of life, of death, of judgment. He called men to follow him in a radical, "no middle ground" type of way.

His claims about himself, and those made by his followers, cannot be ignored. The Jews of his day took up stones to stone him because they recognized the implications of his words.[133] They knew he was speaking as no prophet of old had spoken, and just like those living today, they had to make a decision. Follow, or reject him?

When the Jewish leadership could find no body and they were faced with witness after witness to his resurrection, they tried to suppress the message of Christ. But this only spread the message far and wide as persecuted Christians took the message of a risen Christ to the far corners of the known world. They filled Jerusalem first with the gospel message and then "turned the world upside down" with their preaching about Jesus. The eyewitnesses remained in the church, teaching and preaching, all the way to the point in time when the Gospels themselves were written, providing a consistent, geographically broad testimony to the core of the Gospel message. These Gospels stand firmly upon the martyr testimonies of those early Christians who refused to compromise on the message, "Jesus is risen! Repent and believe!"

One of the stories about the risen Christ that was treasured by those early generations of believers is found in the final chapter of Luke. If you have taken the time to read *The Jesus Family Tomb*, or even to scan

---

[133] See my work, *The Forgotten Trinity* (Minneapolis: Bethany House Publishers, 1998) for a biblical defense of the deity of Christ.

through some sections of such works as *The Acts of Philip*, I strongly urge
you to take a few moments to consider this record, written long before
an ascetic in Asia Minor came up with the name "Mariamne," and walk
the road to Emmaus with those two disciples of old:

13 And behold, two of them were going that very day to a
village named Emmaus, which was about seven miles from
Jerusalem. 14 And they were talking with each other about all
these things which had taken place. 15 While they were talking
and discussing, Jesus Himself approached and *began* traveling
with them. 16 But their eyes were prevented from recognizing
Him. 17 And He said to them, "What are these words that you
are exchanging with one another as you are walking?" And they
stood still, looking sad. 18 One *of them*, named Cleopas,
answered and said to Him, "Are You the only one visiting
Jerusalem and unaware of the things which have happened
here in these days?" 19 And He said to them, "What things?"
And they said to Him, "The things about Jesus the Nazarene,
who was a prophet mighty in deed and word in the sight of
God and all the people, 20 and how the chief priests and our
rulers delivered Him to the sentence of death, and crucified
Him. 21 "But we were hoping that it was He who was going to
redeem Israel. Indeed, besides all this, it is the third day since
these things happened. 22 "But also some women among us
amazed us. When they were at the tomb early in the morning,
23 and did not find His body, they came, saying that they had
also seen a vision of angels who said that He was alive. 24
"Some of those who were with us went to the tomb and found
it just exactly as the women also had said; but Him they did not
see." 25 And He said to them, "O foolish men and slow of
heart to believe in all that the prophets have spoken! 26 "Was it
not necessary for the Christ to suffer these things and to enter
into His glory?" 27 Then beginning with Moses and with all the
prophets, He explained to them the things concerning Himself
in all the Scriptures.

28 And they approached the village where they were going,
and He acted as though He were going farther. 29 But they
urged Him, saying, "Stay with us, for it is *getting* toward evening,
and the day is now nearly over." So He went in to stay with
them. 30 When He had reclined *at the table* with them, He took
the bread and blessed *it*, and breaking *it*, He *began* giving *it* to

them.   31 Then their eyes were opened and they recognized Him; and He vanished from their sight.   32 They said to one another, "Were not our hearts burning within us while He was speaking to us on the road, while He was explaining the Scriptures to us?"   33 And they got up that very hour and returned to Jerusalem, and found gathered together the eleven and those who were with them,   34 saying, "The Lord has really risen and has appeared to Simon."   35 They *began* to relate their experiences on the road and how He was recognized by them in the breaking of the bread.

36 While they were telling these things, He Himself stood in their midst and said to them, "Peace be to you."   37 But they were startled and frightened and thought that they were seeing a spirit.   38 And He said to them, "Why are you troubled, and why do doubts arise in your hearts?   39 "See My hands and My feet, that it is I Myself; touch Me and see, for a spirit does not have flesh and bones as you see that I have."   40 And when He had said this, He showed them His hands and His feet.   41 While they still could not believe *it* because of their joy and amazement, He said to them, "Have you anything here to eat?"   42 They gave Him a piece of a broiled fish;   43 and He took it and ate *it* before them.

44 Now He said to them, "These are My words which I spoke to you while I was still with you, that all things which are written about Me in the Law of Moses and the Prophets and the Psalms must be fulfilled."   45 Then He opened their minds to understand the Scriptures,   46 and He said to them, "Thus it is written, that the Christ would suffer and rise again from the dead the third day,   47 and that repentance for forgiveness of sins would be proclaimed in His name to all the nations, beginning from Jerusalem.   48 "You are witnesses of these things." (Luke 24:13-48)

The disciples on the road to Emmaus had not just moved Jesus' body to a second tomb. They had not marked a year on their calendar so that they could go back and collect his bones. They were confused, for they realized that there was a fundamental contradiction between the promises he had pointed them to in the Scriptures and the idea that he was dead and buried. But now, reports that he had risen! Notice that they do not yet understand what these things mean. These are not schemers plotting to start a new religion! These are not liars who are so hardened in their deceit that they will die a martyr's death just to maintain the lie. When Jesus joins them, he walks with them and points them to the prophecies of old and their fulfillment in himself. How unlike the Jesus of the Gnostics, the Jesus of *The Acts of Philip!* The true Jesus fulfills the Scriptures, he continues the prophetic line and completes it, and he directs his followers to the Scriptures.

Every believer in Jesus Christ has walked to Emmaus, each in his own way. Each of us can testify that we have had our minds opened to see the beauty and consistency of the Scriptures, and their testimony to Jesus Christ. And we have come know him who conquered death and the grave, and lives forever more. Many of us walked the streets of skeptical Toronto, and, for a time, mocked those who headed off toward Emmaus. But then, by God's grace, our hearts were changed, and we could no longer find satisfaction where we were. By grace we journeyed to Emmaus, and we invite you to make the journey as well. It may seem a long and difficult road, but, when you are joined by the one who conquered death, the journey is filled with purpose and joy.

And by the way...the road to Emmaus leads *away* from Talpiot. Those who walk it know they are leaving nothing behind, for that temporary tomb borrowed on the dark Day of Preparation was empty on the morning of the resurrection. Indeed, Christians down through the ages join the testimony of Scripture and the facts of history:

"He is not here! He is risen!" (Luke 24:6)

Summary of Errors, Problems, Contradictions, and Half Truths in the Tomb Theory

- The book and film were not subjected to serious scholarly examination prior to release to the public.

- Many scholars cited in the film and book have affirmed that they were not told the full story, and that their statements have been used out of context.

- The theory uses double standards in its tremendously inconsistent use of the New Testament, at times accepting its accuracy on one point, then rejecting it on the next, without following any logical standards.

- The film and book demonstrate a consistent willingness to document only particular facts related to its conclusions, ignoring those facts that are contrary to its conclusions.

- The central argument of the film (that "Mariamne" is the original name of Mary Magdalene) is subject to numerous counter-arguments and explanations.

- The inscription on the Mariamne ossuary can be read at least three ways, and the first two, which leave the entire theory without any ground, are more likely than the third, upon which the theory depends.

- Even taking the inscription as the theory does, there is no reason whatsoever to believe a fourth century work of fiction, *The Acts of Philip,* is relevant to first century Jerusalem.

- *The Acts of Philip* nowhere refers to, or identifies Mariamne as, Mary Magdalene. The name Mary Magdalene never appears in *The Acts of Philip.*

- *The Acts of Philip* say Mariamne could turn into an ark of glass and a pillar of fire. Do the theorists think Mary Magdalene could do this?

- The film misrepresents Francois Bovon of Harvard who has confirmed that he is only referring to the Mariamne/Magdalene connection in the realm of literary parallels, not history.

- Bovon refers to the theory's claims that Jesus and Mary Magdalene had a child as "science fiction."

- The film misrepresents even the existing text of *The Acts of Philip* by saying the book says Mary Magdalene (which it never mentions) would be buried in Jerusalem. It actually says Mariamne would die in the Jordan River (which does not flow through Jerusalem).

- The theory's willingness to abandon first century documents directly related to Jesus and his original followers (the New Testament) in favor of a work of fiction from the Encratite community of Asia Minor three hundred years later is a clear indication of its bias.

- The film and book misrepresent the nature and capacities of forensic mitochondrial DNA testing.

- Simcha Jacobovici claims Carney Matheson concluded that the genetic testing shows Yeshua bar Yosef and Mariamne were married. Matheson denies this conclusion forcefully.

- Mitochondrial DNA testing can only address maternal relationships, not paternal ones. Hence, the two genotypes tested could have included a father/daughter relationship, a fact inexplicably left out of the discussion by the film and book.

- The names of Jesus, Mary, Joseph, etc., have been found in other burial sites in Jerusalem in the past, including *Dominus Flevit*.

- All of the names in the Talpiot tomb are found amongst the top ten most popular names for men and women in the time period of the first century in Jerusalem.

- The argument that there is at least a 600:1 chance that this is the "Jesus family tomb" is based upon the assumption that 1) there is a Jesus family tomb in Jerusalem, and 2) it has been found. That is, the statistical argument assumes its own conclusion so as to have validity!

- There is no reason whatsoever to believe Jesus would own a multi-generational tomb in Jerusalem. He was from Nazareth, 120 miles to the north, in Galilee, and only visited Jerusalem.

- The theories propounded in the book concerning the Knights Templar are presented without even the pretense of factual or historical foundation, and as such, have as much validity as *The Da Vinci Code*. They are pure fiction.

- The alleged "cross" symbol on the Jesus ossuary is far more likely the simple "this side forward" mark to indicate which way to slide the lid so that it would fit.

- The idea that the Judah, son of Jesus in the Talpiot tomb is the author of the Gospel of Thomas, which was written in AD 165, a century after the Talpiot tomb was sealed, is emblematic of the kind of scholarship represented in *The Family Tomb of Jesus*.

- The film and book desperately seek to avoid honestly stating the only possible ramification of their theory: that Christianity's primary claim in the resurrection of Jesus Christ is false, and hence Christianity is a false religion.

Obviously, many more examples could be culled from the preceding pages of documentation and discussion (ignoring the second Joses in the

New Testament, turning Simon Peter into two men, etc), but this should be sufficient to share with those who wish a quick answer to the question "does the tomb theory have credibility?"

On the Resurrection

In the fall of 2005 I had the privilege of engaging John Dominic Crossan in debate in Seattle on the historical reliability of the Gospels.[134] A few days later, while at sea on the Ms. Mercury, a four-man debate took place on the subject of the resurrection. Dr. Crossan was joined by Dr. Marcus Borg, and I was joined by Dr. Jim Renihan of Westminster Seminary in Escondido, California. Given the time constraints of the venue, each man gave a ten-minute opening statement, and this was followed by discussion and dialogue between the members of the panel. Given the relevance of the topic to the tomb story, I here provide the transcripts of the opening statements by myself and Dr. Renihan.

James White: the NT Witness to the Resurrection

When Paul wrote to the Corinthian believers in the first half of the sixth decade, around A.D. 54, he included in his letter some of the most primitive Christian tradition known to us. Specifically, in 1 Corinthians 15 he presents an early creedal statement summarizing the gospel of Jesus Christ. These words surely predate Paul; that is, he himself says these words were passed on to him, and so we must push their composition to within a matter of a few short years, barely a decade, after the events of the ministry of the Lord Jesus Christ. These are not the words of a later generation reflecting and redacting, they are the words of the most primitive era of Christianity. And here we read:

> ³ For I delivered to you as of first importance what I also received, that Christ died for our sins according to the Scriptures, ⁴ and that He was buried, and that He was raised on

---

[134] The audio and video recordings of this debate are available at www.aomin.org.

the third day according to the Scriptures, [5] and that He appeared to Cephas, then to the twelve. [6] After that He appeared to more than five hundred brethren at one time, most of whom remain until now, but some have fallen asleep; [7] then He appeared to James, then to all the apostles; [8] and last of all, as to one untimely born, He appeared to me also (1 Cor. 15:3-8).

Now please note what Paul here relates. The most primitive message of the faith speaks of the death of Jesus Christ for our sins, a phrase of substitution using the term ὑπέρ (*huper*); we know the death of Christ was a historical event and the term "death" here is being used in its normative sense. Next, the faith says he was buried, and once again there is no reason to think of this term in any other sense than the normative one that would naturally flow from the preceding historical term, "died." And then the earliest faith of Christianity says He was raised on the third day according to the Scriptures. The term used here, ἐγείρω (*egeiro*), is the third in a chain of terms that we have seen are being used in their normative sense. Jesus was raised from the dead in fulfillment of Scriptural prophecy. The meaning of the term in this context is unambiguous; it flows naturally from what precedes, and, of course, flows of necessity into what follows, that being the post-resurrection appearances of the Lord.

I emphasize these basic facts for the simple reason that our debate today truly turns on whether we will allow the Scriptures to define their own teaching, through their own language and native meaning, or whether we will choose to reject the testimony of the apostles and instead embrace a foreign meaning to these words that is more amenable to a post-modern world or a foreign theological paradigm. For I truly do not believe that there is any question at all of what the New Testament means when it says to us that Jesus Christ rose from the dead. It means that the body of Jesus Christ was buried after his crucifixion; that that body was dead, expired, deceased. And that on the third day, that body left the grave, not metaphorically, not allegorically, not mythically, but bodily, physically, in an incorruptible yet truly physical form. Indeed, Paul continues from this point to address the question of the nature of the resurrection body simply because he has to do so in light of the resurrection of Jesus Christ.   If the Corinthian believers accepted his message, then they would naturally ask what kind of body believers would receive at their own resurrection. As Paul taught earlier in this letter, "Now God has not only raised the Lord, but will also raise us up through His power" (1 Cor. 6:14). The Christian message is that because Jesus Christ has been raised from the dead, we too will be raised from the dead. The power of death has been broken, eternal life is ours, only in and through Jesus Christ. And so it is natural for believers to wonder about the nature of that resurrection body.

Now surely if the Corinthians had missed Paul's point, he would have stopped them immediately and said, "No, you are asking the wrong question. There is no resurrection body, for resurrection is merely spiritual; the body decays and is gone and is never seen again, and you need to realize that when we say Jesus rose from the dead all we mean is that he was taken up to God and absorbed into him or that his apostles are continuing his program, his kingdom, here on earth, and that is how he is 'present.'" But this is precisely what Paul does not do. Instead, he uses words and phrases in contexts that communicate with blunt and undeniable force the physicality of the resurrected Jesus.

And so I would like to first insist that we need to be shown examples of *egeiro* used in similar contexts—i.e. relating to the historical death of Christ or someone else, in the context of Tannaitic Judaism, which clearly, as we see in the gospels, possessed a belief in a physical resurrection—wherein the term refers either to a mere remembrance of a person and their program, or where it refers not to a physical resurrection, but to an exaltation and absorption into God himself.

Next, I would assert that the term "resurrection" points to this same conclusion. "Raised" from the dead is *egeiro*, but another term appears, that being ἀνάστασις (*anastasis*), from *anistemi*, which likewise clearly and forcibly in the context of the New Testament refers to a physical resurrection, that which died coming to life again. The lexical sources are united on this matter. Listen to the words of Paul:

> 12 Now if Christ is preached, that He has been raised from the dead, how do some among you say that there is no resurrection of the dead? 13 But if there is no resurrection of the dead, not even Christ has been raised; 14 and if Christ has not been raised, then our preaching is vain, your faith also is vain. 15 Moreover we are even found to be false witnesses of God, because we testified against God that He raised Christ, whom He did not raise, if in fact the dead are not raised. 16 For if the dead are not raised, not even Christ has been raised; 17 and if Christ has not been raised, your faith is worthless; you are still in your sins. 18 Then those also who have fallen asleep in Christ have perished. 19 If we have hoped in Christ in this life only, we are of all men

most to be pitied. [20] But now Christ has been raised from the dead, the first fruits of those who are asleep (1 Cor. 15:12-20).

Clearly, Paul moves effortlessly back and forth between the term "raised" and that of "resurrection." As my brother Dr. Renihan will demonstrate, the natural use of this term in Paul's preaching found in Acts likewise proves his meaning as well. Paul says, "if there is no resurrection of the dead, not even Christ has been raised," demonstrating the same truth concerning resurrection as we saw regarding the idea of being raised from the dead. There is also no way to avoid the salvific meaning of the death of Christ latent in this passage. Indeed, to hope in Christ, for Paul, is to hope in the risen Christ, not in a Christ concept, not in a memory.

Surely the testimony to the resurrection contained in the canonical gospels themselves is fully consistent with this apostolic writing which we can firmly date as to its writing to A.D. 54; all the discussions of Q gospels or second-century Gnostic gospels simply cannot overthrow the preserved testimony to the belief in substitutionary atonement and physical resurrection so plainly and forcefully found in Paul's Corinthian literature.

And yet, despite this forceful presentation, there are some who miss Paul's point and focus upon a later phrase he uses so as to in essence completely overturn his teaching. I refer to 1 Corinthians 15:42-44:

[42] So also is the resurrection of the dead. It is sown a perishable body, it is raised an imperishable body; [43] it is sown in dishonor, it is raised in glory; it is sown in weakness, it is raised in power; [44] it is sown a natural body, it is raised a spiritual body. If there is a natural body, there is also a spiritual body.

Some have focused upon the assertion, "it is sown a natural body, it is raised a spiritual body," as if this is a denial on Paul's part of the physical nature of the resurrection. But this is clearly an error that can be demonstrated both by examination of the context as well as the actual terms Paul uses. When we follow the context we see Paul's point: in the resurrection the glorious nature of the resurrection body is likened to four pairs of contrasting terms: perishable/imperishable; dishonorable/glorious; weak/power; *soma psuchikon/soma pneumatikon*. I gave the last pair in the original tongue so as to avoid importing concepts not found in the original. The contrasting pairs are not, I repeat, not indicating "physical/non-physical," so there is no reason at all to assume that the fourth pair all of a sudden breaks out of the context to make this kind of assertion. But even more so, the terms Paul uses proves this as well. The contrast is between "soulish" and "spiritual." Paul had used the same term, "soulish," in 1 Corinthians 2:14, where he says the natural, or soulish man, does not discern the things of the spirit of God. So he is not talking about a physical man versus a non-physical man, but a natural, unregenerate, earthy man versus the regenerated, spirit-led man; likewise, the contrast in 1 Corinthians 15:44 is not between a physical body and a spiritual body, but between a natural, earthy body, subject to corruption, and a spiritual, spirit-animated, incorruptible body, that of the resurrection. If we simply look carefully at the terms and the context, we can discern Paul's meaning.

And so I conclude that the testimony of the Scriptures is very clear: the terms are plain, the lexical sources united, the contexts compelling. Our hope is in a risen Christ, and if we have no risen Christ, then we are, as Paul rightly said, of all men most to be pitied.

Dr. Jim Renihan on the Witness of the Book of Acts

The text is of importance for our discussion. Now I would like to focus on the text of the book of Acts, an historical record of the spread of Christianity, and a demonstration of how Christians, writing one generation after the event of the resurrection, actually viewed that event. Now by my count we have reference to the resurrection of Jesus nearly thirty times in that book. These occurrences surround three key terms and their cognates: ζωή (*zoe*), ἀνίστημι (*anistemi*), and ἐγείρω (*egeiro*). Now we can only take a furtive glance at these three terms in a couple of texts where they appear, but they are greatly enlightening.

The first of them is in Acts 1:3. Luke, in the introduction to this book, when he writes to Theophilus (whoever Theophilus may have been), speaks about Jesus in the past and Jesus in the present, and he wants to remind Theophilus of the earlier book, which we call the Gospel of Luke. He says this in his third verse: "to whom He also presented Himself alive after His suffering by many infallible proofs, being seem by them during forty days, and speaking of the things pertaining to the kingdom of God." Now we notice that Luke uses the language of "presenting Himself alive," ζῶντα (*zonta*), "after His suffering." And in this word Luke introduces a theme that will be central to his presentation, and he does so in such a way that no one is able to mistake his terms. Now you notice he doesn't use either of the words that typically are used to speak of resurrection; he speaks about life, and he uses the word that typically refers to "living being." The use of *zonta* makes this point, and it is buttressed by citing the reality of witnesses and infallible proofs. F.F. Bruce, for example, tells us that Aristotle wrote that the word we have translated as "signs" means "a compelling sign; something that gave demonstration." Now this text cannot be understood in any other way but in terms of a physical resurrection of Jesus' body after His sufferings. Luke says He was alive, and He demonstrated that He was alive, and that sets the tone for all of the rest of the discussion of resurrection in the book of Acts.

Now the second passage I would like to turn to very briefly is in Acts 17. I wish that we could work our way through all of the different texts in the book of Acts, but there are two places in Acts 17 that are of interest for our discussion. For example, when Paul comes into Athens, having reasoned in the synagogue, he also goes into the marketplace. And we are told that there were certain Epicurean and Stoic philosophers who encountered him, and they said, "'what does this babbler seem to say?' while others said 'He seems to be a proclaimer of foreign gods' because he preached to them Jesus and the resurrection." Later on, during the same visit to Athens, Paul stands in the center of Greek philosophy, in a place called the Areopagus. And there in the Areopagus, he speaks to his audience about who Christ is. And when he comes down to the end, he says this: "'God has appointed a day on which He will judge the world in righteousness by the man Whom He has ordained. He has given assurance of this to all by raising Him from the dead.' And when they"—that is, the Greek philosophers—"when they heard of the resurrection of the dead, some mocked, while others said 'We will hear you again on this matter.' So Paul departed from among them." Now notice the reactions that Paul receives when he speaks about the resurrection—explicitly related to the resurrection of Jesus. Why did he receive such mocking responses? Well, if the resurrection does not describe a physical resurrection, what would have been the basis for the words and behavior of his opponents?

Thirdly, we look at Acts chapter 23, where Paul, after being taken prisoner in the city of Jerusalem, is allowed to speak to the Jewish high council, the Sanhedrin. And Paul perceived that there were two different parties present before him, the Pharisees and the Sadducees, and so he says "I am a Pharisee, the son of a Pharisee. Concerning the hope and resurrection of the dead I am being judged." And Luke tells us "When he had said this, a dissension arose between the Pharisees and the Sadducees, and the assembly was divided. For Sadducees say that there is no resurrection, and no angel or spirit, but the Pharisees confess both." Now we're all aware of this division between Sadducees and

Pharisees. But Paul exploits it. And it could not be more clear how he exploited it and why he did so. The Pharisees, who believed in a physical resurrection, at this time, strangely, came to his defense. And the Sadducees were offended by the words that he spoke.

Very quickly, the fourth text that I want to look at is in Acts chapter 26, where Paul, in the continuing narrative of the events that follow Acts 23, is now in Caesarea standing on trial or in defense of himself before Festus, the Roman governor, before Agrippa, the puppet king of Israel, before dignitaries from the city of Caesarea, before Agrippa's court and Festus' officers. And he comes and he speaks to them plainly and clearly about the resurrection. Early on in his speech he asks this poignant question: "Why should it be thought incredible by you that God raises the dead?"

A Word to Atheists and Materialists

You do not believe in God. I do. You probably think you've heard just about every argument there could be for the existence of God, and yet you remain unconvinced. Do not worry. I shall not take your time with a further rehearsal of what you have already rejected. Don't get me wrong: I believe that there is not only sufficient evidence to demonstrate the existence of God, but there is an over-abundance of such evidence. I do not believe in God without evidence. I do not live in a dream world, disconnected from reality. I believe reality cannot be interpreted consistently and logically outside of the recognition of God's existence. You disagree. You don't see any evidence for God at all, and can only think that my belief in God is some mental projection, possibly instilled in me during my youth, or the result of an inability to cope with stresses as an adult.

Be that as it may, I would like to invite you, if you will, to think with me for a moment about what I believe. Surely that is not too much to ask. Even if you continue in your disbelief, at least you will know a little better why I think, and act, as I do. Besides, I assert that my world view (my belief system, if you prefer) is internally consistent. Yes, I am concerned about consistency, logic, rationality. I believe that for man to recognize the existence of God is not only perfectly rational, but is the only truly rational position to take. But I'm getting ahead of myself.

I am a Christian theist. I can speak only of a Christian world view. I do not find consistency in any other system of theistic belief. To say that I am a Christian theist is to say that I believe that there is only one God. He has revealed Himself to be personal, infinite, timeless. He is not simply a "higher power" but a personal being, who wills, acts, and communicates. He is infinite in that He is not limited in any way: spatially, or temporally. He is timeless in that He is the creator of time itself. He does not undergo a progression of events, but exists outside the realm of time. As a Christian theist I believe that God is the creator of all that is. He is the ground of being of all that exists. Nothing exists that does not owe its being every second to the power and will of God.

As a Christian theist, then, I believe in a personal infinite, and eternal God who has revealed Himself in certain ways. God has revealed Himself in the creation around me, He has revealed Himself in the Scriptures, and most importantly He has revealed Himself in the God-man, Jesus Christ. I know you don't believe that any of these ways of "revelation" are valid or sufficient—I don't expect you to. I'm just explaining where I'm coming from.

Since God is the Creator, then man is His creation. I believe that every breath I take, every beat of my heart, every second of my existence is utterly dependent upon the power and will of God. He sustains me continuously. All men, according to the Christian world view, owe everything they are to God. They are God's creation, He their Creator. Any view of man, then, that does not take into consideration the Creator/creation relationship is contrary to the Christian position.

"Enough," you may say. "All of that is just fine if you want to believe it, but just leave me out of it." I understand your hurry to move on to other things, especially if you have already decided that all religions are little more than the inventions of men to assuage their primitive fears or meet some kind of psychological need. You may be surprised to know that in the vast majority of cases, I agree with you. We could quite profitably discuss the quantum differences between the religions of men and biblical Christianity, but that is not my purpose now.

We go back to our original comments. "Where is the evidence for belief in such a God? " you may ask. "I've seen it all, and remain utterly unconvinced." I don't doubt it. I have encountered more than one atheist who is very intelligent and well read who said the same thing. So what's the point?

May I suggest that if what I believe is right—if you really are the creation of God—then you might do well to consider the wisdom of your demand for evidence of the existence of God, as well as your disbelief therein? What I mean is this: if you owe your very existence to God (can you utterly disprove that you do?), then it becomes obvious that the creature is not wise to reject the existence of its creator. It would be somewhat like a computer denying that it had a human creator, all the time asserting that it 'finds no evidence' of the existence of such a being. All it sees around it is its own little universe of chips, disks, and programs. Since there are no human beings within its view, it then might conclude that there was no such thing.

It would seem an obvious truth that atheistic sentiments are foolish if such a God as the one of which I speak exists. But that is just the point, isn't it? You don't believe such a God exists. And we are back to the issue of evidence. You just don't see sufficient evidence to believe that the Christian God exists. But I do. Why the difference? I recognize the existence of intellect and intelligence in you, and hopefully you are not one of those atheists who relegates all "religious people" to the scrap heap of stupidity. So why can two people, such as you and I, look at the same world and come up with such completely different conclusions at such a basic level?

I believe the answer lies in the starting point of our thinking. You and I don't start at the same place. If God exists, then I simply cannot begin with myself as the starting place of my thinking. And why not? Does one start with the created, finite, limited, and dependent being, or with the uncreated, infinite, unlimited, and independent being, upon which all else is dependent both for existence and, I would assert, for meaning? I don't see myself as sufficient to be the starting place and foundation of my thinking. If God exists, then any system of thinking must be predicated upon Him, not on something less. On the other hand, you do consider yourself as a sufficient starting place. In fact, you assert that there cannot possibly be any other foundation of thought outside of yourself. You must begin with you, and, I would assert, you will then end with you. But don't you see what all of this means? I cannot join you on your foundation, on your starting point, because it automatically, from the very beginning, denies the existence of God! How so? If you start reasoning out from yourself in an attempt to 'find' God, then you are denying that you are a created being, dependent upon God in all things. You will surely never find the Christian God in this way. For me to join you on your human starting-point is for me to deny what I believe—that I am the creation of God, and no sufficient foundation for human thought or predication can be found outside of Him.

"But this is all circular!" you might say. "You begin with the existence of God!" Yes, that's right. And I'm up front about it. I admit it. But my friend, you too are in the same boat! I have my particular set of unprovable presuppositions. But so do you! I assume my createdness. You assume your non-createdness! I assume my dependence upon God. You assume your independence from God.

Any system of thought has to have, at its foundation, a set of unproven and unprovable assumptions, presuppositions if you like, that give form and substance to all that follows. The most 'rationalistic' system of philosophy, at its foundation, has unproven assumptions that its adherents accept without evidence. Christians are often faulted for the concept of 'faith,' yet no matter what system of philosophy you may hold, you hold to its foundational aspects by faith. You have your set of presuppositions, and I have mine. That is why we see things differently.

Take the issue of "evidence" as an example. You claim you find no evidence for the existence of God. I claim there is a great deal. If what I have said is true, then you have basically set yourself up as judge, jury, and prosecuting attorney in the case of "Me vs. God." Though you certainly have no right to act as judge of God, being His creation, you do so anyway. Since this is obviously an act of rebellion, then you must commit a good deal of energy into making the whole thing work. So, you demand of God (or of those who would speak to you of Him), "Show me the evidence! I shall judge! " Though it is not your position to judge anyway, you demand the evidence all the same. Now, if you were to allow into evidence anything that would demonstrate the existence of God, you would, by default, be letting go of the thing you hold most dearly—your autonomy, your independence from God. You would have to step down from the judgment seat and take your proper position as the created being rather than the independent judge. So, to avoid this plight, you simply dismiss any and all evidence that could in any way cause you to have to recognize the existence of God. Despite my providing you a lengthy list of evidences for God, my efforts would be in vain. "Case dismissed for lack of evidence" would be your verdict.

I see you are shaking your head. Stay with me long enough to recognize that if you are truly God's creation, then what I have said is true. You have no right to judge God—only He has the right to judge you! Your assumed ability to act as judge, to begin with yourself and determine, in your rebellion, what is and what is not 'sufficient' evidence in your eyes to establish the existence of God is really nothing more than a desperate attempt to hide your denial of the nature of your very own being behind a cloak of 'rationality' and skepticism. It is the ultimate act of denial, a smokescreen with eternal consequences.

Will you step down off of the bench and relinquish the robes of judgment to the proper Judge? If God is working in your life, opening your blind eyes, giving understanding to your mind, you will. I invite you to call upon God for His mercy and to forgive you for taking to yourself what is His by right. If He shows mercy to you, what I have said will make perfect sense. But, for many others, it will only be more religious double-talk. I am not God, and I cannot say to whom God will be merciful and who He will leave in their own self-imposed darkness. I can only ask you to carefully consider my words, and seek the truth of God in the Scriptures.

The Christian Message

The content of the Christian message is found in the book that Christians believe was given by God as a revelation of Himself—the Bible. The Bible tells us things about God that we could not know otherwise. What follows is based solely and completely on that book.

What is God Like?

The Bible's message begins with God.[1] The Bible does not argue God's existence—it simply states it, assuming that man knows that God exists.[2] In fact, the Bible says that the created universe around us is sufficient to demonstrate the existence of God.[3]

The Bible says there is only one God.[4] He is the Creator of all that is.[5] He is not a part of creation, but is distinct from creation, for He existed prior to the created universe, and was under no compulsion to bring the universe into existence. God is spirit and has always been— He never "started" at some point in time. He is eternal.[6] Because God has created all things, and because God Himself is personal and creates with a reason, then all things have purpose and meaning. God is holy.[7] He is the absolute standard of goodness itself—there is nothing evil or corrupt in God.[8] Because He is holy, He must punish evil.

God is personal—in fact, the Bible tells us that God is tri-personal; that is, that the one being of God is shared by three eternal persons: the Father, the Son, and the Holy Spirit. This would be contradictory if we said that God was one being and three beings, or one person and three persons, but as long as one remembers that being and personality are different things, the Bible's teaching is quite clear.[9] And, though it is one of the greatest mysteries of all, we are told that God is loving, merciful, and kind[10]—and that despite man's rebellion against Him!

The Problem with Man

One of the main problems with man is the fact that he refuses to see himself as God sees him. God has given us guidelines by which we can see if we are "functioning" properly. Many of these guidelines have to do with how we behave—such things as that we should worship only the one true God,[11] that we should not murder[12] or commit adultery,[13] steal[14] or lie.[15] The Bible wraps up all of these commandments by giving us the highest standard—"You shall love the Lord your God with all your heart and with all your soul and with all your strength and with all your mind; and, You shall love your neighbor as yourself."[16] Any honest individual, when faced with God's standard, will admit to falling short. The Bible calls this rebellion, or sin. All have sinned—none can escape that charge.[17]

Sin separates from God, and as God is the source of all life, the result of sin is death[18]—physical death on this earth as well as spiritual death—alienation from God both now and in eternity. God's wrath is revealed against sin, and hence against sinners.[19] Man, separated from God, even while physically alive, is spiritually dead, incapable even of seeking after God.[20]

Man, on his part, tries desperately to escape encountering the Holy God. He does this by suppressing the truth that he can see all around him. He becomes self-centered and self-seeking, turning the worship that should belong to God inward upon himself, or upon some other created object.[21] Every conceivable sin finds its origin in the condition of man as sinner.

God's Means of Saving Man

God could have simply executed the punishment of the law upon rebellious man—but He didn't. God does not owe man even the first chance at salvation—God is under no obligation to man at all. Yet, He has not left us in our lost situation. He has an eternal plan to bring the greatest good out of man's evil. That plan is wrapped up in a person—the person of Jesus Christ.

Jesus Christ was completely unique—He was not simply a prophet or a good man, He was God the Son in human flesh—the God-man.[22] He was totally without sin[23]—He perfectly obeyed all of God's law. Hence, He was not under the curse of death. Death had no power over Him. Yet, He died. Why?

Jesus voluntarily laid down His life as a substitute.[24] Since He did not have to die, He voluntarily took the place of all those who believe in Him throughout the ages. By dying in their place, He took their punishment upon Himself—He died their death so that they can live His life. In fact, the Bible says that God sees us as if we died with Christ upon the cross of Calvary![25] Since the penalty of sin is death, and Christ has died that death, then sin is forgiven for all those who die with Christ! This is how God has decided to bring about forgiveness of sins—in the death of Jesus Christ. Hence, all sin will be punished—either on the cross of Calvary, or in eternal hell. Where one's sins will be punished is dependent upon whether one is in Christ Jesus or not.

God has decided to save a people for His own sake.[26] In His grace He has joined these people from all eternity to Jesus Christ, so that His death is their death.[27] Jesus did not die indiscriminately for everyone—He died only for those who believe in Him. Not only this, but the Bible says that on the third day after His death, Jesus rose from the dead—He was resurrected, never to die again.[28] And, since those who are saved died with Christ, they also have the promise of being raised up with Him in eternal life.[29]

But who are these who are "in Christ" or who have died with Him? How can a person avail himself of this great plan of salvation? Doesn't the Bible say that man does not even seek after God?[30] Yes, it does say that. The answer is found in the very grace of God. God's grace is something He gives because He wishes to give it, not because we earn it, merit it, or buy it. Man has no claim upon God's grace. Grace, by definition, is given freely.[31]

Jesus taught, "No man is able to come to Me unless the Father, who sent Me, draws him, and I will raise him up at the last day."[32] Man, being dead in sin, is given new life simply on the basis of God's desire to do so. And to whom does God give this life? The Bible calls them "the elect," which simply means that these people, no more deserving than any others, are chosen by God, completely on the basis of His own will and mercy, to be united with Christ, forgiven of their sins, and given eternal life.[33] Once God has given to them spiritual life which the Bible calls "regeneration" or being "born again."[34] He also gives to them the gifts of repentance[35] and faith.[36] Man responds to these actions of God by repenting and believing in Christ. But God's choice of these people is based completely upon grace and mercy—nothing else.

Trusting Christ

What does it mean when the Bible speaks of a person "believing" in the Lord Jesus Christ? It is far more than simply an intellectual acknowledgment that Jesus is Lord and Savior—though that is a vital part of it. It also involves a commitment to Him as Lord in one's life—

a willingness to turn all of one's life, including one's dreams, goals, and ambitions, over to the Lord Jesus, to follow Him wherever He leads. This kind of commitment can only come from the work of God in man's heart, as we have already seen.

"But," one might say, "if God is the one who saves, and it is only on the basis of His mercy that anyone can be saved, how can I personally be saved?" If the true desire of your heart is to trust in the Lord Jesus Christ and to commit yourself to Him as your Lord and then as your Savior, such a desire can only be placed in your heart by the Spirit of God.[37] "What, then, must I do?"

"Believe on the Lord Jesus Christ, and you will be saved" is the Bible's answer.[38] In faith toward the Lord Jesus, and a heart-felt desire to turn from anything which is against God's will, commit yourself to the Lord Jesus, knowing that His death is sufficient to cleanse you from all your sin. Hold only to the Lord Jesus and nothing else—trust Him to save you and give to you eternal life. He has promised to do so.[39] Pray a heartfelt prayer of repentance and commitment. God has promised, "Every one who calls upon the name of the Lord will be saved."[40]

Some Questions Answered

1) Can we earn salvation? Certainly not—man, being dead in sin, is unable to save himself, or to contribute anything toward his own salvation. God's way is to save completely and fully in Jesus Christ, and in no other way. Any other teaching is not the Gospel of Jesus Christ.[41]

2) Are there any too sinful to be accepted by Christ? No, none at all. Each of us was at one time dead in sin before we were raised up by God.[42] The sacrifice of Jesus Christ is sufficient to cleanse from all sin.[43]

3) But what of the cost of following Jesus? Yes, there is a cost—not a cost to being saved, but a cost of living as a disciple of Jesus Christ. He calls us to live a holy life, separate from the sinful attitudes of the world.[44] The standards of Christian living are very different than those of the world. As men and women who have died with Christ, our outlook on life should be different—the glory of God should be our highest priority, rather than the fulfilling of personal desires.[45]

4) How can I persevere? What if I fail? When God saves, He does so completely. It is not in our power that we persevere, but in the power of God. It is His promise that He will complete the work He has begun in us.[46] The Bible says, "God, who has called you into fellowship with His Son, Jesus Christ our Lord, is faithful."[47] It is the faithfulness of God that brings about the faithfulness of the Christian.

What Next?

The Bible speaks of Christ's "church." The church, in its most general sense, is not a single organization or group or denomination—it is the entire company of God's elect that is to be found in every organization that worships God, teaches and preaches the Bible, and leads others to the true Jesus Christ. It is vital that you find a local church that believes that the Bible alone is God's Word; that teaches the truth about God and Jesus Christ as seen above. The pastor of such a church would be happy to speak with you about the work the Lord has begun in your life. Also important is the continued study of God's Word, the Bible. Find a good, modern translation of the Bible such as the "New American Standard Bible" or the "English Standard Version" and read from it every day. A good place to start is with the Gospel of John.

[1]Genesis 1.1-2 [2]Psalm 14.1 [3]Romans 1.18-20, Psalm 19.1 [4]Deuteronomy 6.4, Isaiah 43.10, 44.6-8, 46.9-10, Psalm 86.9-10 [5]Genesis 1.1, Colossians 1.16-17, John 1.3, Jeremiah 10.12 [6]John 4.24, Psalm 90.2 [7]Isaiah 6.3, 5.16, Psalm 99.3, 5, 9 [8]1 John 1.5, Psalm 92.15 [9]This teaching is based on three Biblical truths: A) There is one God Isaiah 43.10; B) There are three divine persons described in Scripture Matthew 3.16-17, 28.19-20, and C) Each of the divine persons has equality with the others Colossians 2.9, John 20.28. [10]Psalm 86.15, Lamentations 3.22-23 [11]Exodus 20.3-4, Exodus 34.14 [12]Exodus 20.13 [13]Exodus 20.14 [14]Exodus 20.15 [15]Exodus 20.16 [16]Luke 10.27 [17]Romans 3.10-18, 23, Ecclesiastes 7.20 [18]Romans 6.23, Ezekiel 18.4 [19]Romans 1.18, John 3.36 [20]Ephesians 2.1-14, Colossians 2.13, Romans 3.11 [21]Romans 1.21-25 [22]John 1.1-18, 1Timothy 3.16, Colossians 2.9, Philippians 2.5-11 [23]1 Peter 2.22, Hebrews 4.15 [24]John 10:14-18, 2 Corinthians 5.21, 1Peter 3.18, Isaiah 53.4-6 [25]Galatians 2.20, Romans 6.1-10 [26]Titus 2.14, Matthew 1.21 [27]Ephesians 1.4-6, Romans 8.31-34 [28]Luke 24.1-16, 1Corinthians 15.3-8 [29]John 5.24, Romans 6.8-10 [30]Romans 3.11 [31]Romans 11.6, Ephesians 2.8-9 [32]John 6.44 [33]John 6.37-40, Romans 8.28-9.24, Ephesians 1.3-11, 2 Timothy 1.9 [34]John 3.3-6 [35]Romans 2.4, 2 Timothy 2.25 [36]Ephesians 2.8-10, Romans 12.3 [37] Romans 8.5-8 [38] Acts 16.31 [39]John 5.24, 6.40, 8.12 [40]Romans 10.13 [41]Romans 4.1-5, Galatians 1.6-9, 2.21, 3.24 [42]Ephesians 2.1-6 [43]1 John 1.7 [44]1 Peter 1.13-16, 1 John 2.15-17 [45]Romans 6.11-18, Colossians 2.7-8 [45]Philippians 1.6, 1Corinthians 1.30-31, John 10.25-29, Romans 5.1-2 [47]1 Corinthians 1.9

Bibliography

Bauckham, Richard. *God Crucified*. Grand Rapids: Eerdmans, 1998.
_____. Jesus *and the Eyewitnesses: The Gospels as Eyewitness Testimony.*
Grand Rapids: Eerdmans, 2006.
_____. *Gospel Women: Studies of the Named Women in the Gospels.*
Grand Rapids: Eerdmans, 2002.
_____. *Jude and the Relatives of Jesus in the Early Church.* Edinburgh:
Clark, 1990.

Bovon, Francois, B. Bouvier, F. Amsler. *Acta Philippi. Textus.* Corpus
Christianorum, Series Apocryphorum 11. Turnhout: Brepols,
1999.
_____., A. Brock, C. Matthews, eds. *The Apocryphal Acts of the
Apostles.* Harvard Divinity School Studies. Harvard, 1999.

Evans, Craig A. *Fabricating Jesus: How Modern Scholars Distort the Gospels.*
Downer's Grove: IVP Books, 2006.

Ilan, Tal. *Lexicon of Jewish Names in Late Antiquity: Part I: Palestine 330
BCE-200 CE.* TSAJ 91; Tubingen: Mohr, 2002.

Kloner, Amos. "A Tomb with Inscribed Ossuaries in East Talpiyot,
Jerusalem." *Atiquot* XXIX, 1996, 15-22.

Komoszewski, J., M. James Sawyer, Daniel Wallace. *Reinventing Jesus:
What the Da Vinci Code and Other Novel Speculations Don't Tell You.*
Grand Rapids: Kregel Publications, 2006.

Magness, Jodi. "Has the Tomb of Jesus Been Discovered? SBL Forum, 2007. http://www.sbl-site.org/Article.aspx?ArticleId=640

Patrologia Latina [CD-ROM]. Alexandria, VA: Chadwyk-Healey, 1995.

Pfann, Stephen. "Mary Magdalene is Now Missing: A Corrected Reading of Rahmani Ossuary 701." March, 2007. http://www.uhl.ac/MariameAndMartha/

Price, Robert M. *Deconstructing Jesus.* Amherst, NY: Prometheus Books, 2000.
_____, *The Incredible Shrinking Son of Man.* Amherst, NY: Prometheus Books, 2003.

Rahmani, L. Y. *A Catalogue of Jewish Ossuaries in the Collections of the State of Israel.* Jerusalem: Israel Antiquities and Israel Academy of Sciences and Humanities, 1994.

Roberts, A., and James Donaldson, eds. *The Ante-Nicene Fathers.* Grand Rapids: Eerdmans, 1982.

Rollston, Christopher A. "Prosopography and the Talpiyot Family Tomb: Pensées of a Palaeographer." SBL Forum, 2007. http://www.sbl-site.org/Article.aspx?ArticleId=649

Tabor, James D. *The Jesus Dynasty: The Hidden History of Jesus, His Royal Family, and the Birth of Christianity.* New York: Simon & Schuster, 2006
_____. "Two Burials of Jesus of Nazareth and the Talpiot Yeshua Tomb" SBL Forum, 2007. http://www.sbl-site.org/Article.aspx?ArticleId=651

Thesaurus Linguae Graece [CD-ROM]. Irvine, CA: University of California, 1992.

BURNING ISSUES TITLES

In addition to *From Toronto to Emmaus* we are delighted to offer the following books in our new *Burning Issues* series:

YEARNING TO BREATHE FREE? *Thoughts on Immigration, Islam and Freedom*
by David Dykstra

This provocative book was recently featured in WORLD Magazine (October 28, 2006).

PULPIT CRIMES: *The Criminal Mishandling of God's Word*
by James R. White

This thought-provoking book is the perfect gift to give to the local pastor who has been compromising the pulpit against his own conscience. Vital for the pulpit and the pew!

TWO MEN FROM MALTA: *A Passionate and Rational Appeal to Roman Catholics*
by Joe Serge and Joel Nederhood

A newspaperman from Canada and a pastor with a worldwide radio and television ministry team to present the truth of God's Word to thoughtful Roman Catholics who want the truth.

COMMON FAITH & COMMON CULTURE: *How Christianity Defeats Paganism*
by Joe Bianchi

Wayne Mack says of this book, "I commend this book to you and encourage you to buy it and then read it through at least twice and share it with others."

Printed in the United States
73379LV00002B/472-525